Zora Neale Hurston
— ON —
FLORIDA FOOD

Zora Neale Hurston

— ON —

FLORIDA FOOD

RECIPES, REMEDIES & SIMPLE PLEASURES

FRED OPIE

AMERICAN PALATE

Published by American Palate
A Division of The History Press
Charleston, SC 29403
www.historypress.net

Copyright © 2015 by Frederick Douglass Opie
All rights reserved

First published 2015

Manufactured in the United States

ISBN 978.1.62619.872.2

Library of Congress Control Number: 2014953425

Notice: The information in this book is true and complete to the best of our
knowledge. It is offered without guarantee on the part of the author or The
History Press. The author and The History Press disclaim all liability in
connection with the use of this book.

CONTENTS

INTRODUCTION

There is enormous variety in American cookery. This book focuses on Florida cooking in Zora Neale Hurston's early twentieth-century ethnographic research and writing. It emphasizes the essentials of cookery in Florida through simple dishes. It considers foods prepared for everyday meals as well as special occasions and looks at what shaped the eating habits of communities in early twentieth-century Florida. It investigates African, American, European and Asian influences in order to understand what they contributed to Florida's culinary traditions.

This book analyzes barbecuing, basting, smoking, roasting, frying and the use of traditional ingredients such as rice, cornmeal, pork, poultry and fish. It also explores the links beyond Hurston's native Eatonville, looking at the people, places and cookery throughout Hurston's literary and ethnographic writings. It studies the cookery of West Florida, Jacksonville and the Everglades.

This book builds on the pioneering work of Jessica Harris, Karen Hess, Howard Paige, Sidney W. Mintz, Arjun Appadurai, Pete Daniels, Andrew Warnes and Mark Kurlansky. Like Warnes's work, this one delves into Hurston's writing, offering a fascinating perspective on African cultural survival strategies in the twentieth century and the culinary links between Floridians and blacks in other parts of the Americas. Warnes focuses on *Their Eyes Were Watching God* and Eatonville, making no comparisons to the cookery in West and Central Africa. This book makes comparison with food history gathered from a number of sources. Warnes's analysis focuses only on barbecuing and basting. This book's emphasis is more expansive, analyzing various cooking methods. It also considers Hurston's discussion of food in Florida in the context of West and Central African culinary history, and it parallels Hurston's foodways with Pete Daniels's work on lowdown culture and this author's work on soul.

Daniels argues that lowdown culture is a pleasure-seeking, working-class culture practiced by relatively autonomous single men and women— roustabouts, as it were. These men and women search for high wages and have plenty of time for lowdown leisure, namely eating, drinking, gambling and sexual activity. Soul is the style of rural folk culture. Soul is spirituality and experiential wisdom. Soul is finding a way to endure and survive with dignity. Soul food has been influenced by other cultures and is enjoyed by a global community of historically rural folk.

This book is divided into five chapters in roughly chronological order. The first chapter looks at Hurston's family history and foodways in early twentieth-century Alabama and Florida. Chapter 2 delves into African American foodways in Florida and the essential staples of it. Chapter 3 discusses the recording of natural food remedies and unpacks their history and applications of many decades. Chapter 4 talks about the centrality of poultry, especially fried chicken, in Florida's culinary history. Chapter 5, the final chapter, talks about barbecue as a technique and event and examines the social and political aspects of barbecue that few writers on the topic get into.

Period recipes are shared throughout the book from cookbooks and black newspapers. Such newspapers informed communities about recipes, many of which African American cooks and food writers from around the country collected and tested. Generally, each black neighborhood had a local distributor of black papers who sold subscriptions to the *Philadelphia Inquirer*, the *Pittsburgh Courier*, the *Chicago Tribune*, the *New Journal & Guide*, the *Afro-American* and the *New York Amsterdam News*. These newspapers kept black readers informed about food trends and recipes from Florida and its bordering states. Careful attention has been given to using geographically and historically relevant recipes from cookbooks and historical newspapers to Hurston's life and work and using Hurston passages to introduce recipes, which solidifies their connection to Hurston's writings.

This book evolved from an intensive two-year project. I am thankful to Babson College and those staff and administrators who provided the support to complete the project—particularly Carolyn Hotchkiss, Donna Bonaparte and Paula Doherty. Thanks also to Henry Louis Gates Jr., the staff of the

Hutchinson Center for African and African American Research and my colleagues at the center during my 2012–13 fellowship year at Harvard University. I learned and continue to learn so much from a brilliant and collaborative group of scholars I worked with during my year at Harvard. Thank you to the research assistants who made important contributions to completing the book—Ana Paula Marinovic, Tandra Taylor and Rachel Taylor. And as a writer with ADHD, special thanks to my editors, Tracy Quinn McLennan and Cynthia Ramnarace. Research for the book was done at Harvard, the special collections at the Beinecke Library at Yale University and the Library of Congress. I spent my fellowship year writing at Harvard and completed the first draft of the book in one year. My productivity was aided immensely by the excellent research assistants and editors I collaborated with who allowed me to crank out chapter drafts and make revisions.

Chapter 1

A HUNK OF CORN BREAD

Zora Neale Hurston was born in wintertime, the season when southerners butchered hogs and harvested sweet potatoes. One of the first voices she heard was that of a white man calling, "Hello, there! Call your dogs!" But what follows isn't the story you'd expect from the late nineteenth-century Jim Crow South.[1]

As a child born in Alabama, Hurston heard the story of "a white man of many acres and things, who knew the family well, [and] had butchered [some hogs] the day before" her mother went into labor. "Knowing that Papa was not at home, and that consequently there would be no fresh meat in our house, he decided to drive the five miles and bring a half of a shoat (a young pig), sweet potatoes, and other garden stuff along. He was there a few minutes after I was born," writes Hurston. Seeing the front door open, he came in and announced his presence in what Hurston called "the regular way to call in the country because nearly everybody who has anything to watch has biting dogs."[2]

Nobody responded, but he heard the newborn crying. He shoved the door open, rushed in and followed the sound until he found Hurston's mother, Lucy Ann Potts. The umbilical cord was still attached. "Being the kind of a man he was, he took out his Barlow knife and cut and tied the umbilical cord," writes Hurston.[3] When the midwife arrived almost an hour later, she found a fire made in the stove, hot water simmering on the stove and Hurston's cleaned-up and bandaged mother holding a recently cleaned off

Farmers slaughtering hogs, Monticello, Florida, circa 1930. *Courtesy of State Archives of Florida, Florida Memory.*

Slaughtering time at Hubert Bilinski's place, Jefferson County, Florida, 1927. *Courtesy of State Archives of Florida, Florida Memory.*

newborn in her arms. As soon as the midwife arrived, the white man left the food he had brought and left "cussing about" the local women folk and the midwife not being there to help deliver the baby.[4]

Dating back to the colonial period, rural folk in the South organized days when they slaughtered and butchered hogs. They did this around December or January, using the cold winter weather as a natural refrigerator. Hog killing was a collective community event and often an integrated one in some parts of the South, at least until affordable refrigeration technology became widespread and available after World War II. Slaughtering, butchering and preparing hogs for curing and smoking can best be described as a highly skilled, labor-intensive process. As a result, in most rural societies, hog killing involved all the neighbors, who would butcher and process the meat of six or more hogs at one time. The event would start early in the morning and last late into the evening. Responsibilities would be divided up, with some doing the slaughtering and butchering and making lard for cooking, some making sausage and chops and some preparing choice cuts for curing

Henry White and John Leland (Jack) Hare butcher a hog, 1913. *Courtesy of State Archives of Florida, Florida Memory.*

Hog killing at the Marchant Farm, Newberry, Florida, 1932. *Courtesy of State Archives of Florida, Florida Memory.*

The crew after butchering seventeen hogs on Marchant Farm, Newberry, Florida, 1932. *Courtesy of State Archives of Florida, Florida Memory.*

and smoking hams. Others would clean the intestines for a "chitlin strut," a southern specialty in which the hog intestine is boiled until tender and then battered and deep fried. The women organized makeshift outdoor kitchens where they made hot food to share after the work had been completed and the messy ordeal cleaned up. They cut up the hog skin and dropped the pieces into large cauldrons filled with hot oil to make crackling, the roasted skin of the pig.[5] Women passed the crackling out to the workers along with pans of freshly baked hot corn bread, roasted sweet potatoes and molasses. "It is a gay time" with large pots and skillets "cooking with plenty of seasoning, lean slabs of fresh-killed pork frying for the helpers to refresh themselves after the work is done. Over and above being neighborly and giving aid, there is the food, the drinks, and the fun of getting together," writes Hurston.[6]

The story of Hurston's birth and the ritual of hog-killing season reveal that the food necessities of southern farmers, as well as southern hospitality, at times prevailed over Jim Crow customs and laws. It might seem at odds with common notions of hostile and violent white supremacy; however, oral histories of others who grew up like Hurston in the Deep South around the same period show Hurston's experience was not an anomaly.[7]

LEAVING ALABAMA

Hurston's parents had deep roots in Alabama. The son of a preacher, John Hurston was born in 1861 in Notasulga in Macon County. He remained illiterate into his early twenties.[8] As a young adult, he survived as a journeyman carpenter and agricultural laborer on white-owned plantations. He and others like him lived hand-to-mouth without the ability to save or own much in the way of property or possessions. Like his father, he eventually became a preacher but continued to work as a carpenter.[9] Hurston's mother, Lucy Ann Potts, was born in 1865, also in Notasulga. Her father owned and farmed his own land, including five acres of clingstone peaches. Before marrying, Lucy had received training as a schoolteacher.[10] The two met at a church in Alabama in the late nineteenth century.

Hurston's parents lived as sharecroppers on a cotton plantation in Notasulga. Hurston, the fifth of eight children, was born in Alabama but maintained in her autobiography that she was born in Eatonville, Florida. "Just why Hurston hid her Alabama roots can only be guessed at," writes historian Pamela G. Bordelon. "Her moving from Alabama before the age of two meant that she had little conscious knowledge of the place. Being identified with the all-black town of Eatonville, Florida rather than with the sharecropping and tenant-farming plains of rural Alabama, was more in keeping with the image of herself that she was trying to create."[11]

After Hurston's birth, John set out alone for Florida in search of better opportunities. Eventually, he found them in a newly formed black township called Eatonville in Orange County. He became an ordained Baptist minister, and in 1892, the rest of the family joined him.[12] He went on to pastor several congregations in Florida, including the Macedonia Missionary Baptist Church in Eatonville and Zion Hope Missionary Baptist Church in Sanford. He remained an itinerant pastor in Florida for the rest of his life, a career that kept him gainfully employed and put food on the family's table. Ministers in the rural South commonly led multiple churches, particularly in the Baptist denomination, which had always been the least restrictive in terms of ordination. As a result, the number of Baptist churches far outnumbered other Protestant denomination in the South, and able-bodied ministers remained in demand. Growing up in the home of a preacher meant that Hurston's family fed visiting ministers who came to her father's churches to preach on Sundays or during revival meetings.[13]

In the American South, annual revival meetings, which the Baptists called "protracted meetings" and the Methodists called "camp meetings," became a religious tradition for church folk. Revivals and camp meetings provided opportunities for people to socialize, gather news, worship, evangelize and

A 1940 scene of a church picnic in the U.S. South. *Courtesy of Library of Congress.*

feast on food. Church picnics and all-day preaching and dinner on the grounds became a tradition basic to southern church people (and candidates running for elected office). Local church leaders like Hurston's father and mother would have regularly organized at least one annual weeklong revival that included invited speakers the family would have hosted and fed.[14]

THE HURSTON HOMESTEAD IN EATONVILLE

From all accounts, the Hurston homestead in Eatonville can best be described as almost self-sufficient in terms of the food staples the family depended on for its survival. They lived in a large home with five acres of garden space for growing produce. The garden produced so many "oranges, tangerines, and grapefruit" that during World War I, Hurston and her siblings used the excess "as hand grenades on the neighbor's children."[15]

Collard greens from the family garden were a Hurston family staple. Most families in the South ate them, but women performed the gendered and labor-intensive practice of washing collards and other greens in preparation for cooking them. Cleaning collard greens calls for submerging them in cold water and washing the grit that generally sticks to the leaves over and over again until they are cleaned. A kitchen without running water made the task even harder.[16] Hurston recalls when her "mother was going to have collard greens for dinner," she would take a dishpan full of them "down to the spring to wash the greens."[17] The love affair with eating greens made the process of cleaning them a commonplace activity among the black women Hurston grew up around and later observed while doing fieldwork. One finds dozens of references to greens—kale, collard, turnip and mustard greens—in her letters and published works. Hurston writes about Mrs. Tony Roberts, the "pleading woman" in her hometown of Eatonville, who begged store owner and Mayor Joe Clarke and others for the essential ingredients—greens and salt pork—to prepare greens for her children. "She sing-songs in a high keening voice, 'gimme lil' piece uh meat tuh boil a pot uh greens wid. Lawd knows me an' mah chillen is SO hongry!'" Hurston adds:

> *Sister Pierson* [begged Roberts], *plee-ee-ease gimme uh han'ful uh collard greens fuh me an' mah po' chillen! "Deed, me an' mah chillen is SO hongry. Tony* [my husband] *doan' fee-ee-eed me!" Mrs. Pierson picks a bunch of greens for her, but she springs away from them as if they were*

poison. "Lawd a mussy, Mis' Pierson, you ain't gonna gimme dat lil' eye-full uh greens fuh me an' mah chillen, is you?"[18]

No matter what your color or class, most southerners ate greens. Hurston describes members of the church leadership as "people [who] looked and acted like everybody else—or so it seemed to me. They ploughed, chopped wood, went possum-hunting, washed clothes, raked up backyards and cooked collard greens like anybody else."[19]

Collard Green Recipe

Collard greens
Bacon

Wash collard leaves. They should not be too old and coarse. Cut finely. Boil until extremely tender, a matter of at least an hour, preferably longer—they can scarcely be cooked too long, and are equally good "warmed over"—in enough water barely to cover, with several thin slices of white bacon to each market bunch of the leaves. The water should almost cook away, leaving a delicious broth known to the South as "pot liquor." Cornbread is always served with collard greens and it is etiquette to dunk the cornbread in the pot liquor.[20]

In addition to growing produce, the Hurstons raised hogs and egg-laying chickens. Hurston recalls that "we had all the [hard-boiled] eggs we wanted," and it was "a common thing for us smaller children to fill the iron tea kettle full of eggs and boil them and lay around in the yard and eat them until we were full. Any leftover boiled eggs could always be used for missiles."[21] There was also plenty of chicken and fish.[22] The Hurstons, in other words, rarely went hungry.

Other culinary staples in the Hurston home included canned fruit preserves Lucy Hurston made from the family garden, including quart glass jars full of guava, pear and peach jellies and preserves. Speaking of her family home in Eatonville, Hurston writes, "Downstairs in the dining room there was an old 'safe,' a punched design in its tin doors. Glasses of guava jelly, quart jars of pear, peach and other kinds of preserves."[23]

Demonstrating the canning process at Florida Agricultural and Mechanical College for Negros, circa 1900. *Courtesy of State Archives of Florida, Florida Memory.*

Mrs. J.C. Waldron with preserves in her pantry, Aucilla, Florida, 1939. *Courtesy of State Archives of Florida, Florida Memory.*

Shelves of canned and preserved goods, 1925. *Courtesy of State Archives of Florida, Florida Memory.*

Peach Preserves Recipe

½ box of peach gelatin
6 peaches pared and sliced
2 juiced lemons
2 teaspoons of vanilla

Prepare the gelatin as before (put one-half box of gelatin in cold water, let it stand two hours; add a pint of boiling water and the other ingredients; pour into molds and set on ice to cool), one half dozen peaches (pared and sliced), the juice of two lemons and two teaspoonfuls of vanilla.[24]

Currant Preserves Recipe

Currants
Sugar

Strain juice of raw currants though cheese cloth bags. To every cup of clear juice you must have one cup of granulated sugar heated in the oven; do not allow it to melt. Boil the clear juice for about five minutes then add the sugar until thoroughly dissolved. Just before it comes to a boil, remove from fire and pour into jelly glasses.[25]

Ginger Pear Preserves Recipe

8 pounds hard green pears
8 pounds sugar
½ pound green ginger root
Juice of 4 lemons

Cut the outside skin off the lemons in very small pieces. Be sure to cut away the white part, leaving only the yellow outside skin. Put the ginger root to soak in a pint of lukewarm water over night. Drain off the water, strain and save to put with the sugar. Scrape and cut the ginger in thin slices. Put all the ingredients together and cook nearly an hour or until the syrup is thick.[26]

Watermelon Rind Preserves Recipe

Rind from a large watermelon
Sugar
Juice of two large lemons
Piece of white ginger

Carefully save the white rind and peel it. Cut it into rather long thick pieces, about the size and thickness of a small cucumber pickle. Take the juice and rind of two large lemons and cook with a piece of white ginger until tender. Take the weight of the melon fruit in sugar and enough water to dissolve it. When the syrup has cooked until it ropes; add the lemon juice, rind and fruit. Then cook all together until clear.[27]

Strawberry Preserves Recipe

1 pound firm strawberries
2 cups sugar

To every pound of picked, firm strawberries, allow two cups of sugar. Arrange the berries and sugar in a basin and allow to stand for an hour to extract some juice. Turn them into a preserving kettle, and let come to a boil. Allow to boil for 5 minutes and remove berries with a skimmer. Let the juice boil until thick and pour it over the berries. Let stand until cool, then leave until perfectly cold. Divide into sterilized glasses and pour about a ¼ inch of melted parowax over the contents.[28]

Cherry Preserves Recipe

Morella Cherries (any kind of sour cherry will work)
Sugar

Put the fruit after stoning, into a stone jar. Set in a kettle of water, and cover the jar. Boil slowly for an hour or until the fruit is soft. Put a small quantity at a time in a jelly bag and allow it to drip. To each pint of juice, add one pound of sugar. Pour into a preserving kettle, boil the juice for twenty minutes, add the heated sugar, and boil for 5 minutes. Pour into sterilized glasses and seal with melted Parowax.[29]

SUGAR CANE

Eatonville residents also grew their own sugar cane. In Hurston's culinary South, people chewed sugar cane, and some seemed to have a drug-like addiction to it. She describes the town as a place where all the residents "never stopped cane chewing" in front of locals but concealed the habit in front of northern white tourists.[30] Eatonville native Coon Taylor "couldn't resist [Mayor Joe] Clarke's soft green cane" patch, recalls Hurston. "After he had cut six or eight stalks by the moonlight, Clarke rose up out of the cane strippings with his shotgun and made Coon sit right down and chew up the last one of them on the spot. And the next day he made Coon leave his town for three months."[31] Hurston describes how her uncle Jim would go down to Joe Clarke's general store on payday to purchase "a quart of peanuts and two stalks of sugar cane" on his way to a romantic interlude with a woman at a little house in the woods where there lived "a certain transient light of love."[32]

Eatonville natives did not know this, but cane chewing was also popular among working-class whites up north. A 1924 newspaper report revealed customers in the New York tavern the Pink Pups and Purple Cows "sipping mineral water and chewing sugarcane."[33]

Sugar cane and peanuts served as the box of candy of their day, with suitors purchasing them for their love interests. Hurston writes that on payday in Eatonville, "the town collected at the store-post office on Saturday

The African American section of Belle Glade, Florida, 1937. *Courtesy of Library of Congress.*

A Jamaican laborer cutting cane in the field, Clewiston, Florida, 1947. *Courtesy of State Archives of Florida, Florida Memory.*

nights" and "the men tell stories and treat the ladies to soda water, peanuts and peppermint candy."[34] A townswoman named Daisy, whom Hurston calls "the town vamp," would flirt and try to seduce married men into buying her "some soda water or peanuts" at Joe Clarke's store.[35]

Pork and Corn Bread

No discussion of Florida food history can be complete without talking about grits, home-cured pork and corn bread. A piece of Hurston's corn bread played an important role in her learning how to walk at nine months old. Having recently picked some fresh collard greens from the garden for the evening meal, her mother put them in a dishpan and went down to the spring to wash them. She gave her daughter "a hunk of corn bread to keep [her] quiet" and left her sitting on the kitchen floor. Everything was going along all right until the family's sow "with her litter of pigs in convoy" smelled the corn bread crumbs she had been dropping and scattering across the floor.[36]

The sow began to nuzzle around, coming into the house and making a beeline toward the eating infant. Hurston screamed at the sight of the oncoming hungry sow. Her mother dropped the pan of collard greens and came running back into the house. Hurston recalls:

A sow and her piglets in Sarasota, Florida, circa 1930. Joseph Janney Steinmetz was a renowned photographer whose images appeared in the *Saturday Evening Post* and *Life* and *Time* magazines. His work documented the social history of Floridians. Steinmetz relocated from Philadelphia, Pennsylvania, to Sarasota, Florida, in 1941. *Courtesy of State Archives of Florida, Florida Memory.*

Her heart must have stood still when she saw the sow in there because hogs have been known to eat human flesh. But I was not taking this thing sitting down. I had been placed by a chair, and when my mother got inside the door, I had pulled myself up by that chair and was getting around it right smart. As for the sow, poor misunderstood lady, she had no interest in me except my bread. I lost that in scrambling to my feet and she was eating it. She had much less intention of eating Mama's baby than Mama had of eating hers. With no more suggestions from the sow or anybody else, it seems that I just took to walking and kept the thing a'going.[37]

Corn Bread Recipe

2 cups buttermilk
1 cup molasses
1 tablespoon soda
$^1/_3$ cup water
1 teaspoon salt
2 cups Indian meal
2 cups rye meal (or graham)

Combine buttermilk, molasses, soda dissolved in one-third cupful of water, salt, Indian meal, and rye meal (or graham). Beat well together. Grease four baking pans and pour the above mixture into them. Grease the covers and place lightly over the bread. Steam two and a half or three hours. After steaming, let the loaves stand a few minutes, when they can be lightly shaken out.[38]

THE THREE MS

This story provides important insights into the historic three Ms of southern foodways—meal (cornmeal), meat (salt pork) and molasses—and Hurston's culinary roots. Corn is native to the Americas and was introduced to Africa by Europeans after 1492. In northern Angola and the western Congo, corn became a food complement that proved easier to grow and cultivate than indigenous crops such as sorghum, millet, teff and couscous during environmental catastrophes such as locusts and flooding. By the 1600s, travelers in Africa write about women in the Congo, Angola and São Tomé wrapping corn bread in banana leaves and baking them in the fire cinders. Enterprising women on the coast of Guinea sold corn bread to Portuguese slave traders in local markets.

After they arrived in the Americas, free and enslaved African women continued to make and sell bread made from corn principally because it was readily available as a food ration. Depending on the region, slave owners in the South distributed cornmeal, salt pork and molasses. Access to kitchen utensils, when they had it, and ingredients such as sugar, salt and eggs allowed enslaved cooks to use cornmeal in a variety of ways. They made hoecakes, puddings, dumplings, porridges and corn breads. Hoecakes were made by pouring cornmeal batter onto the blade of a long-handled hoe and baking it over hot cinders. The hoe was brought to the Americas by West and Central African farmers during the Atlantic slave trade.[39] When they ate corn bread and a stew or gumbo together, the corn bread was often used to soak up the liquid, a process referred to as "sopping." Until almost the Civil War, people did not eat with spoons; they ate soups and stews with bread, which they used to sop up one-pot meals.

Northern elites considered corn bread, molasses and fatback (the strip of fat from the back of a hog usually cured by drying and salting) among the "roughest of food" relegated to the people living on the margins of society

Bringing home cornmeal ground from the cooperative mill, 1939. *Courtesy of Library of Congress.*

(such as slaves).[40] Yet even after the Civil War, southerners continued to eat molasses with almost every meal. Most often, it was eaten at the breakfast table with corn bread and pork. Southern cooks used molasses as a cold remedy, condiment and baking ingredient.[41]

FROM THE FARM TO THE STORE

The country store was a community convention in rural Florida and other parts of the South, serving as a credit lending, bartering and commercial trade institution. Historian Marc Levinson, who has written a history of the A&P grocery store chain, tells us that mom-and-pop operations survived

W.J. Lohman Sr.'s dry goods store, Fernandina, Florida, 1889. *Courtesy of State Archives of Florida, Florida Memory.*

Interior of Ripp's dry goods store, Key West, Florida, 1900. *Courtesy of State Archives of Florida, Florida Memory.*

despite the rise of larger grocery chains because they offered much-needed credit for poor, hungry customers.[42]

Grocery stores were popular business ventures because they were an easy enterprise for people with little education and even less capital. If a person lost a job on the railroad or was injured while performing hard labor, becoming a shop owner was as easy as purchasing a how-to book on becoming a grocer and using the sample ordering and bookkeeping forms. Easy credit came from wholesalers who provided inventory to small retailers. Storefronts with upstairs apartments made the grocery store business particularly attractive because families could live above the store.

Most stores displayed their merchandise without prices in a window or behind the counter. Haggling over the final sale price of a bag full of groceries was a common and necessary practice, as shopping at such institutions proved expensive.[43]

General stores, town stores or country stores served as the center of rural communities. They functioned as spaces and places where residents and visitors could purchase items that they did not or could not raise on their own farms, such as molasses, sugar, salt and baking powder/baking soda, as well as snacks used for courting a love interest, such as pickled

Outside the dry goods store, Lake City, Florida, 1910. *Courtesy of State Archives of Florida, Florida Memory.*

T.E. Robarts grocery store at North Marion and West Orange, Columbia County, Florida, circa 1920. *Courtesy of State Archives of Florida, Florida Memory.*

pigs' feet, chewing gum, soft drinks, ice cream and cheese and crackers, among others.

Hurston and her family were no strangers to their local general store. Once in Eatonville, what they did not grow or raise was purchased at nearby Joe Clarke's general store. Those purchases, along with periodic trips to merchants and grocers in larger urban settings, provided the balance of what the family consumed. Hurston's father made trips to Orlando to shop for items such as apples and beef imported from "up North."[44]

In Eatonville, stores like Joe Clarke's also served as spaces where one shared and gathered information on events near and far. As a result, general stores naturally evolved into important spaces for local officials and national and state candidates running for office. In Hurston's novel *Their Eyes Were Watching God,* Joe Starks's store is portrayed as the center of community life in Eatonville.[45] Hurston writes, "Men sat around the store on boxes and benches and passed this world and the next one through their mouths."[46]

Before 1920, a sort of bartering system functioned in which people could exchange the foods they produced with the country store operator for goods

Palace Market in Lincolnville, St. Augustine, Florida, circa 1922. *Courtesy of State Archives of Florida, Florida Memory.*

African American boys eating popsicles in Starke, Florida, 1941. *Courtesy of Library of Congress.*

they could not or preferred not to produce. After 1920, well-stocked grocery stores in urban centers in places like St. Augustine, Starke and Belle Glade provided canned food that radically transformed the lives of the working class. No longer did they have to rely on the hot, labor-intensive work of canning in July and August. By the 1920s, A&P and scores of smaller regionally based competitors such as Crook's had established chains of retail stores in southern cities with their own food systems and networks. By this time, the concept of the locally owned, barter-payment general store was losing ground to the larger, better-financed competitors.

FOOD AS REWARD

Hurston's mother, Lucy, dedicated time to making sure that her children would be well read and educated; thus, by the time Hurston entered the Hungerford School in Eatonville, she read at a level far more advanced than her classmates.[47] One story goes that when Hurston was about eight years old, two white women named Ms. Hurd and Mrs. Johnson from Minnesota visited Hurston's classroom at the Hungerford School. Hurston's teacher, Mr. Calhoun, asked several of the students to read a passage about Plato for the visitors. The passage proved too difficult for all the students except for Hurston, who read it flawlessly. The visitors were so impressed that they asked if Hurston could visit them at their hotel, the Park House, the following day in nearby Maitland. During the visit, the two ladies served Hurston stuffed dates, preserved ginger and other finger foods. They asked her to read a passage from an issue of *Scribner's Magazine*, a cosmopolitan magazine for adults. Again, Hurston read the passage perfectly. As a reward, they gave her a heavy cylinder wrapped with decorated paper and filled with one hundred shiny pennies. The next day, the women sent her a slew of books, and they did so again a few weeks later after they had returned to Minnesota.

The experience impressed upon the young child that her love of books and reading could pay dividends, including rich foods and monetary compensation.[48] Hurston also recalls a story from her childhood in Eatonville in which an adult "took out a peanut bar and gave it to me" to reinforce some desired behavior.[49]

Peanut Bar (or Coconut Bar) Recipe

(FOR CAKE)
1 cup sugar
1 teaspoon butter
2 eggs
½ cup boiling sweet milk
1½ cups flour that has been sifted with 2 teaspoons baking powder

Cream butter and sugar; add whole eggs, beat well, then add milk, flour and baking powder. Bake in a large flat bread pan in a medium hot oven. When done, let cool, cut in bars, and use this filling:

(FOR FILLING)
1 ½ cups powdered sugar
½ cup butter
3 tablespoons cream or milk flavored with vanilla

Spread on bars and roll in finely chopped peanuts or coconut.[50]

At age thirteen, Hurston's world was upended when her mother, Lucy, died in September 1904. (The cause of death is unknown.) This began a tumultuous period in her life from 1905 to 1912 that scholars describe as the missing or lost years. Accurate details of her life do not exist other than from the inaccurate account she provides in her autobiography, *Dust Tracks on a Road*. Her father remarried a younger woman with whom Hurston came to blows. In response, John Hurston sent her and her fifteen-year-old sister to attend the Florida Baptist Academy, a Jacksonville boarding school.[51]

It was in Jacksonville that Hurston's world broadened. She had her first experience with racism and charted a path that brought her to Baltimore and later to New York City, where her culinary experiences crossed race, class and economic lines.

JACKSONVILLE

When Hurston arrived at Florida Baptist Academy in Jacksonville at about the age of thirteen, she was forced to trade the culinary pleasures of farm life for the uninspired and repetitive cuisine of institutional living. She had to get used to eating "the grits and gravy for breakfast." This monotonous menu was a far cry from the elaborate variety of food that her mother used to prepare for her in Eatonville. To keep her culinary sanity, Hurston covertly slipped through a crack in the school fence and bought "ginger snaps and pickles...between meals" at a grocery store across the street from the school.[52] The treatment Hurston received in the white-owned grocery store in Jacksonville exposed her to racism that she had not encountered growing up in and around the all-black township of Eatonville. "Jacksonville made me know that I was a little colored girl," Hurston writes. "I was no longer among the white people whose homes I could barge into with a sure sense of welcome. I [got] a piece of candy

Dinner hour on the docks in Jacksonville, Florida, circa 1910. *Courtesy of Library of Congress.*

or a bag of crackers just for going into a store in…Galloway's or Hill's at Maitland or Joe Clarke's in Eatonville."[53]

Growing up around Joe Clarke's black-owned and operated country store in Eatonville, Hurston seems to have not learned how to treat white store owners. African American youth raised in mixed Jim Crowed townships learned such lessons as a survival skill. Black youth learned from their elders how to show black deference to white grocery store merchants of all ages and genders. As Hurston recalls from her experience in Jacksonville, interacting with strange white store owners and employees could be a degrading and even dangerous experience because you never knew when some volatile white southerner was going to explode.

Hurston attended boarding school in dire financial straits, so it is unclear where she got the money to shop. Her financial situation became so unstable that a school official sent her "to help clean up the pantry and do what I could in the kitchen after school" to help pay off her outstanding school bill.[54] Hurston insists that her father abandoned her in many ways, including financially, after the death of her mother. At the end of her first year, she wrote that her father neither came to pick her up nor provided money for her to return home. She only made it home because a school administrator loaned her the money for her passage to Eatonville via the steamship the *City of Jackson*.[55] She recalls that on the trip a mulatto waiter took pity on her and brought her "slabs of pie and cake and chicken…and sent me astern to eat them."[56]

After dropping out of school at about the age of fourteen, Hurston entered the workforce, serving as a personal maid of an actress in a traveling theater group.

Around 1918, at the age of twenty-seven, Hurston completed her high school graduation requirements at Morgan Academy (Morgan State University today) in Baltimore, Maryland. From there, she went to Washington, D.C., and enrolled at Howard University. Hurston earned an associate's degree from Howard University in 1919. Hurston would later go on to earn a degree from Barnard College in New York. One of Hurston's research papers at Barnard came to the attention of the eminent anthropologist Dr. Franz Boas. He became one of Hurston's most important advisors, mentors and advocates. American literature and Hurston scholar Carla Kaplan writes, "The [1920s] were a particularly interesting time to be working as an anthropologist, especially challenging if you were African American and working on African American culture." Studying with Boas gave Hurston needed cachet and privilege in the academy and among potential funders. "No one was more influential in the field than Boas," says Kaplan. Almost all of the leading American anthropologists of the day—Gladys Reichard, Ruth Benedict, Margaret Mead, Jane Belo, Melville Herskovits—were either associates or students of Boas.[57] Hurston became not only one of the few "academically trained African American anthropologists of her day," says Kaplan, but her training at elite Barnard, where students could take courses across the street from campus at Columbia University, put her at the forefront of her field. Hurston would later write, "What I learned from [Franz Boas] then and later, stood me in good stead when…I prepared to go into the field."[58]

Chapter 2

SOME LOVE COLLARDS/ SOME LOVE KALE

In the late 1920s, Zora Neale Hurston began her career as an anthropologist and writer doing fieldwork in Florida and elsewhere. Hurston, like other African Americans, came from a tradition in which every community had a griot, or storyteller, who had the responsibility to teach the oral history of the older generation to the younger. In her fieldwork, she collected materials based on observations of black migrant workers in sawmill and turpentine camps and made recordings at plantations in Florida. She also researched people in sedentary communities such as her hometown of Eatonville, Florida. The resulting work can best be described as that of a griot rather than a social scientist. Up until this time, white scholars did not see any merit in collecting the kind of folklore that attracted Hurston's attention because they viewed the culture as useless rubbish. Hurston's work provides one of the first documented accounts of the African American Floridian table. Through her writings, both differences and similarities in foodways in terms of class, gender and regions become apparent.

Sound Recording 1
"Halimuhfack" is a juke joint (as spelled jook) song from the east coast of Florida. In this 1939 recording, Hurston explains how she collects and learns songs. June 1939, Florida Folklife, WPA Collections, Library of Congress. Zora Neale Hurston, "Halimuhfack" [Listen Now 2 min 7 sec]: memory.loc.gov/afc/afcflwpa/313/3138b2.mp3

Preparing greens in 1938. *Courtesy of Library of Congress.*

A sawmill in Pasco County, Florida, circa 1900. *Courtesy of State Archives of Florida, Florida Memory.*

Packing celery, Sanford, Florida, 1937. *Courtesy of Library of Congress.*

Sawmill workers eating lunch in 1937. *Courtesy of Library of Congress.*

Above: Turpentine workers gathering rosin in Lake County, Florida, circa 1890s. *Courtesy of State Archives of Florida, Florida Memory.*

Left: Turpentine industry workers, circa 1930. *Courtesy of State Archives of Florida, Florida Memory.*

The term "foodways" explains why you eat what you eat and how that changes over time. Hurston's work shows that foodways are like jazz: they're based on improvisation. Jazz musicians play by ear and from printed music, and then they improvise or give solos. Cooks do the same.

The roots of the African American Floridian table are found in West and Central Africa. The Africans who were brought to Florida used oral traditions, apprenticeships and practice to pass down recipes and cooking methods from one generation to another. They also brought Africans plants with them and incorporated American plants (sweet potato, corn and squash) and European plants (collards) and meat (particularly pork) into their cookery. Before abolition, enslaved Africans in Florida received salted pork and cornmeal as part of their rations. The available records show that sawmill and turpentine camp officials, as well as citrus fruit planters, continued these rations or exploited laborers by forcing them to purchase groceries for inflated prices at company commissaries.

PORK

In Eatonville, Hurston talks about a man buying a pickled pig's foot for someone he wanted to court. She provides an example of this in her novel *Their Eyes Were Watching God*, which is based on her experiences growing up in Eatonville and, more than likely, observations made while conducting fieldwork. She writes, "Jim Weston had secretly borrowed a dime and soon he was loudly beseeching Daisy to have a treat on him. Finally she consented to take a pickled pig foot on him."[59]

Why pigs' feet? Since the introduction of hogs from Europe, poor folks who could not afford to throw away any source of protein developed an affinity for the pig parts slaughterhouses discarded. They learned to prepare them in multiple ways, turning parts like pigs' feet into inexpensive and delicious special occasion foods eaten on New Year's Day. Folks with money have always eaten "high on the hog" and held poor cuts like pigs' feet in contempt. In contrast, over the years, the tradition of rural poor folk called for cooking, among other dishes, hog head, pigs' tails and pigs' feet on New Year's Day.[60] Pickled pigs' feet would go on to morph into a popular southern snack. You could purchase them in corner stores and juke joints along with other food items, soft drinks, beer and moonshine.[61]

A grocery store window in an African American section advertising cornmeal and pig parts such as chitlins/chitterlings (intestines) and hog maws (cheeks), 1942. *Courtesy of Library of Congress.*

Before the advent of modern refrigeration, chitterlings (pigs' intestines) had been a seasonal food associated with wintertime hog killing. Like collards and others greens, chitterlings' preparation required tedious cleaning three or more times to remove all dirt (like with greens) and straw, hair, feces, fat and other items a human should not eat (like with hogs); pigs have been known to eat just about anything! Most boil the chitterlings and then clean them with hot water. Then you cut them into smaller pieces. Traditionally, Floridians and other southerners have cooked them with heavily seasoned water in a large covered pot for about three hours until the organ meat breaks down and becomes tender, adding water to the pot if necessary to prevent the intestines from burning. Recipes for seasoning the water vary across the Americas. A typical southerner might use one large chopped Vidalia onion, one-half to one cup of regular or apple cider vinegar, one to two large garlic cloves, three to five large thyme leaves, a quarter cup of lemon juice, one tablespoon of fine ground sea salt and two tablespoons of lemon pepper. Chitterlings served as the least expensive byproduct of the slaughtered hog. But their delicious vinegary, hot and spicy preparation for wintertime holiday meals caused most to view them as a delicacy.[62] Communities hosted popular "chitlin struts," food festivals with chitterling eating at the center that were also served with side dishes.[63] In short, chitlins would have been a natural at a wintertime event like a toe party (see page 90 for more information on toe parties) or chitlin strut.

In 1929, sawmill and turpentine laborers in Florida worked seven days a week with one day off per year for Christmas. As rations, they received "peas, corn bread, and fat meat," according to a 1929 article.[64] The same year, a newspaper reported that turpentine camps in Taylor County, Florida, operated commissaries that sold "grits, rice, canned goods, and no fresh vegetables" at prices "50 to 100 percent higher than at other stores," and the cost of meat at the commissaries remained out of reach for the average worker.[65]

Workers with a log at Page sawmill, Greenville, Florida, circa 1930. *Courtesy of State Archives of Florida, Florida Memory.*

Hurston's anthropological work shows that these workers might have starved if they did not supplement the niggardly allotment of rations that employers distributed to them and/or sold at high prices in company commissaries. Even in otherwise oppressive living and working conditions such as debt peonage, African Americans used African cultural survival skills such as foraging, hunting and fishing for food as part of improvising their foodways.

FISH

Hurston's 1948 novel, *Seraph on the Suwanee*, is an account of an all-black township located near citrus plantations in West Florida. Like her other writing, the novel is based on her fieldwork. She says, "The people raised nothing but vegetables to eat," bred hogs and fished on the Suwanee River:

> *They knew that there were plenty of black bass, locally known as trout, in the Suwanee, and bream and perch and cat-fish. There were soft-shell turtles that made a mighty nice dish when stewed down to a low gravy or the "chicken meat" of those same turtles fried crisp and*

Lewis Plantation turpentine still, Brooksville, Florida, circa 1930. *Courtesy of State Archives of Florida, Florida Memory.*

Loading green turtles for shipping, 1898. *Courtesy of State Archives of Florida, Florida Memory.*

brown. Fresh water turtles were a mighty fine article of food anyway you looked at it. It was commonly said that a turtle had every kind of meat on him. The white "chicken meat," the dark "beef," and the in-between "pork." You could stew, boil, and fry, and none of it cost you a cent. All you needed was a strip of white side-meat on the hook, and you had you some turtle meat.[66]

Floridian Fried Turtle Recipe

FOR EGG BATTER
½ cup flour
$^1/_8$ teaspoon salt
5 tablespoons milk
2 egg yolks, beaten
2 teaspoons olive oil (or Wesson oil)
2 egg whites beaten stiff

Discard the entrails, the liver and eggs, if any, being retained. Slip the clawed feet in boiling water until the tough skin and claws can be slipped off from the meat. The meat is then cut in pieces two to four inches in size and parboiled until thoroughly tender. Add three-quarters teaspoon salt when partly done. Drain. Dip each piece separately in egg batter. Drop batter-covered turtle in deep very hot fat, or in very hot fat to cover in a deep iron skillet. Soft-shell cooter is prepared in the same way, except that the gelatinous outer edge of the soft shell is scalded until the thin skin can be rubbed off, then cut in two- to four-inch pieces and parboiled with the meat. It is dipped also in the egg batter and deep fried. It has an utterly delicious texture and flavor, but is somehow so rich that no more than two portions should be eaten, under penalty of indigestion.[67]

On paydays in a sawmill camp in Loughman, Florida, laborers served fried fish at Saturday outdoor fireside dances.[68] Hurston tells us that typically men caught the fish and cleaned it, and women cooked it. She describes "happy houses" as those in which "hot grease began to pop" as they fried a batch of freshly caught catfish, perch or trout.[69] Hurston recorded an elder in a work camp instructing some young men on how to properly eat fried fish. The story illustrates the popularity of fried fish among African Americans in Polk County. Gene Oliver, one of the younger men, asked Jim Allen to explain the correct way to fry fish. "First thing you chooses a piece of corn-bread for yo' plate whilst youse lookin' de platter over for a nice fat perch or maybe it's trout," says Allen.[70] Put one fish at a time on your plate, with your fork, start at the tail and eat the meat all the way up to the head with some

Men and boy with turtles caught on a trotline, Clermont, Florida, 1905. *Courtesy of State Archives of Florida, Florida Memory.*

corn bread. "Not a whole heap of bread—just enough to keep you from swallerin' de fish befo' you enjoy de consequences." Then turn the fish over and start on the other side. "Don't eat de heads. Shove 'em to one side till you thru wid all de fish from de platter, den when there ain't no mo' fish wid sides to 'em, you reach back and pull dem heads befo' you and start at de back of de fish neck and eat right on thru to his jaw-bones."[71] He concludes, "If it's summer time, go set on de porch and rest yo'self in de cool. If it's winter time, go git in front of de fireplace and warm yo'self—now Ah done tole you right. A whole heap of people talks about fish-eatin' but Ah done tole you real."[72] Hurston recorded another story from a camp laborer named Joe Wiley that also illustrates the centrality of fish on rural Floridian tables. This story comes from her fieldwork in Polk County:

> *Ah knows a man dat useter go fishin' every Sunday. His wife begged him not to do it and his pastor strained wid him for years but it didn't do no good. He just would go ketch him a fish every Sabbath. One Sunday he went and just as soon as he got to de water he seen a great big ole cat-fish up under some water lilies pickin' his teeth with his fins. So de man baited*

his pole and dropped de hook right down in front of de big fish. Dat cat grabbed de hook and took out for deep water. De man held on and pretty soon dat fish pulled him in. He couldn't git out. Some folks on de way to church seen him and run down to de water but he was in too deep. So he went down de first time and when he come up he hollered—"Tell my wife." By dat time de fish pulled him under again. When he come up he hollered, "Tell my wife—" and went down again. When he come up de third time he said: "Tell my wife to fear God and cat-fish," and went down for de last time and he never come up no mo.[73]

Fried Fish and Hush Puppies Recipe
Serves 3 to 4

FOR HUSH PUPPIES
1 cup cornmeal
2 teaspoons baking powder
½ teaspoon salt
1 small to medium onion, minced
1 egg
¼ cup milk or water

Mix together the dry ingredients and the finely cut onion. Break in the egg and beat vigorously. Add the liquid. Form into small patties, round or finger shaped. Drop in the deep smoking fat in which the fish has been fried until they are deep brown. Serve hot and at once.[74]

Black elites, or, as Hurston called them, "well-mannered Negroes," groaned when they observed poor folk eating in public "with their shoes off, stuffing themselves with fried fish," she says.[75] Historically, black women in urban centers across the Americas turned to selling fried fish as street vendors to make money because it required little in the way of supplies, equipment, licenses or formal training. A prime location and a catchy signature cry like "Melt-in-your-mouth fresh-caught hot fried fish!" were the secrets of success.

CORN

Maize or corn is from the Arawak, one of three Amerindian groups to inhabit the Caribbean, from which the word *mahiz* comes. Corn represented the staple grain that Amerindians across the continent cooked with. They used it in a variety of ways, including preparing corn breads, popped corn, puddings, dumplings, porridges, stews and drinks—some of them alcoholic and some nonalcoholic. Native Americans also processed corn by adding ash to make hominy; grinding it into grits and/or meal; and eating it fresh, parched, boiled, baked, steamed and roasted. The Portuguese brought corn to the African continent during the Columbian exchange. Corn flourished in African fields because it was more productive than traditional African crops like sorghum. Africans adapted corn to a number of local recipes for breads, puddings and other dishes. After they arrived in the Americas, Africans continued to make various types of foods and drinks using cornmeal they raised in gardens or received as rations.[76]

Grits made from corn are one of the foods native to the Americas that became a staple of the African American table. In *Seraph on the Suwanee*, Hurston describes a workday table with grits "piled high" on plates served with "fried ham," eggs and coffee.[77] Hurston also describes grits as a central part of the "old-fashioned Sunday breakfast." On Sunday mornings, a pot of savory grits "on the back of the stove all ready and waiting" was a common sight. Grits arrived on the table along with piping hot homemade biscuits shoved in the "oven at the last minute" served with a "quart bottle of molasses" and a "dish of country butter" for the biscuits and grits. The grits and biscuits served as the side dish for a well-

Little AMERICANS *Do your bit*

Eat Oatmeal-Corn meal mush-Hominy - other corn cereals - and Rice with milk. *Save the wheat for our soldiers.*

Leave nothing on your plate

UNITED STATES FOOD ADMINISTRATION

World War I U.S. government war poster, 1917. *Courtesy of Library of Congress.*

World War I U.S. government war poster, 1917. *Courtesy of Library of Congress.*

Payday for Florida East Coast Railway employees in Plantation Key, Florida, 1906. *Courtesy of State Archives of Florida, Florida Memory.*

seasoned tender slab of steak and gravy fried in a "big black iron skillet." The steak would have been "salted, sprinkled over heavy with black pepper, and beat and beat [with a hammer] until it was tender, then doused in flour and dropped into the hot pan to fry," says Hurston, adding that there would also be "thick brown steak gravy with onions in it to go with the grits."[78]

Payday dances at a sawmill camp in Polk County had a reputation for corn-based moonshine (and folk songs). People got drunk on "coon dick" (bootleg moonshine) made out of "grape fruit juice, corn meal mash, beef bones, and a few mo' things," says Hurston. Similarly, in *Seraph on the Suwanee*, she says fruit pickers traded a case of corn "for a gallon of moonshine" and also bartered work in exchange for a barbecue, which included, among other items, "ten gallons of moonshine at a dollar and a half a gallon."[79]

Farmers increased their profits when they fermented corn into moonshine. Camp residents consumed corn as an alcoholic beverage and as a food staple in various forms, from hoecake to soufflés. In the Everglades Cypress Lumber Company camp, "Nearly every skillet is full of corn bread" and every "dinner bucket" had a piece of hoecake.[80]

Orange pickers in Ormond, Florida, circa 1880s. *Courtesy of Library of Congress.*

Confiscated bootleg paraphernalia, circa 1920. *Courtesy of Library of Congress.*

Florida Hoecake Recipe
Serves 3 to 4

1 cup white cornmeal
½ teaspoon salt
2 teaspoons butter or margarine
Water

Mix salt and cornmeal. Pour into it, stirring constantly, enough boiling water to make a batter that just holds together without spreading when placed on the grill. Grease the skillet with butter. Spread batter in one large cake or in smaller cake and grill like pancakes.[81]

Florida Corn Soufflé Recipe
Serves 6

1 can corn or 2 cups cooked corn cut from the cob
1 teaspoon salt
1 tablespoon sugar
2 cups heavy cream
1 tablespoon cornstarch
3 eggs
4 tablespoons butter, melted

Preheat oven to 400° F. Drain the canned corn, if using. Combine salt, sugar, heavy cream, and cornstarch, making sure the cornstarch is fully dissolved. Add to the corn, followed by the well-beaten eggs and melted butter. Turn into a buttered casserole dish and bake for 45 minutes.[82]

PEANUTS

Peanuts are indigenous to Brazil. Like corn, the Portuguese introduced them to West and Central Africa in the fifteenth century. Later, the Portuguese used them as rations on slave ships. Seeing an economic opportunity, African farmers began planting them in their fields and selling them to those

Peanut patch, 1900. *Courtesy of Library of Congress.*

provisioning ships for long journeys. In Africa and the Americas, peanuts became something of a candy that people regularly snacked on.[83] Elite blacks who considered peanuts common or poor folks' food hated seeing working-class blacks on trains and buses "with their shoes off, stuffing themselves… with peanuts and throwing" the shells on the floor, Hurston writes.[84]

Men used peanuts as part of their courting rituals. At the toe party Hurston attended, one finds "hot peanuts" among the list of treats a man could buy for a woman. Apparently, those in charge of the liquor served peanuts with moonshine. Hurston says, "The raw likker known locally as coon dick was too much. The minute it touched my lips, the top of my head flew off. I spat it out and [ate] some peanuts."[85] Peanuts show up in the lyrics of a song sung by Ella Wall, whom Hurston calls "the Queen of love in the jooks [juke joints] of Polk County, Florida." In one of her songs, Wall says, give me "more dancing, drinks, peanuts, [and] singing."[86] On paydays in a sawmill camp of the Everglades Cypress Lumber Company in Loughman, Florida, Hurston found "parched [roasted] peanuts" as part of the refreshments laborers served at a Saturday outdoor fireside dance.[87]

RICE AND BEANS AND PEAS AND RICE

The dynamic duos of rice and beans and peas and rice have their roots in the Akan, Aja, Yoruba and Igbo kitchens in Ghana, Senegal, Nigeria and Gabon. When Africans arrived in the Americas, they continued cultivating these crops, so rice and beans dishes can be found throughout the African diaspora: red beans and rice; Hoppin' John (black-eyed peas and rice); black beans and rice; and pigeon peas and rice. The popularity of these dishes as staples and special occasion foods continued after the abolition of slavery.[88]

In the seventeenth century, West Africans from Cape Verde to the Gold Coast cultivated large amounts of rice. They grew so much rice, in fact, that

A worker enjoying a bowl of rice and beans, 1938. *Courtesy of Library of Congress.*

they became known as the people of the Rice Coast. White rice planters in the South sought out West Africans for purchase as slaves because of their knowledge of rice cultivation. These West Africans brought their methods of cooking long-grain rice with them to the colonial South. The African cook made her greatest culinary mark on areas like Savannah, where blacks outnumbered Europeans. Mulatto rice is evidence of diasporic links between Africa and several regions of the Americas.[89] Hurston begins and concludes her classic novel *Their Eyes Were Watching God* with rice and bean dishes. While Janie tells her friend Phoebe about how her grandmother escaped from slavery in Savannah and migrated first to Atlanta and then to West Florida, Janie is enjoying a plate of mulatto rice. "Mah mulatto rice ain't so good dis time. Not enough bacon grease, but Ah reckon it'll kill hungry," says Phoebe. "Ah'll tell you in a minute," Janie says, lifting the cover off the plate. "Gal, it's too good. You switches a mean fanny round in a kitchen."[90]

Mulatto Rice Recipe
Serves 3

6 *strips bacon*
½ *cup onions, minced*
2 *cups water*
1 *cup tomatoes, diced*
1 *cup rice*

Fry bacon in a pan then remove the bacon and brown a minced onion in the bacon grease. Next, add diced tomatoes. After it is hot, add a pint of rice to the mixture, and cook slowly until the rice is done.[91]

In Polk County labor camps, Hurston found "nearly every skillet" had a pot of black-eyed peas, seasoned with smoked pork, cooking on it. Laborers carried black-eyed peas with them to work in a dinner bucket containing leftovers from the evening meal.[92] Beans were so popular that people sang about them. Hurston recorded a song with one refrain that says, "I don't want no cold corn bread and molasses/I don't want no cold corn bread and molasses/Gimme beans, Lawd, Lawd, gimme beans."[93] Newspaper sources from the same period show that laborers in sawmill and turpentine camps, as well as on plantations, ate beans as one of their staples.

Hurston collected a trickster tale in the South about workers and beans. It goes like this: Three men went to court a real pretty girl with shiny black hair and coal black eyes and a very old and wise father. They all went to her father to ask her hand in marriage. He looked them over, but he couldn't decide which one would make the best husband for his daughter. So he told them, "Be here tomorrow morning at daybreak, and we will have a contest. Whoever can obtain food in the fastest way with trickery, wit and skill can marry my daughter." The next morning, the first suitor noticed that there wasn't any water in the bucket to cook breakfast. So he told the girl's mother to give him the water bucket and he would go to the spring and get her some. He took the bucket in his hand, and then he found out that the spring was ten miles off. But he said he didn't mind that. He went on and filled the bucket with water and carried it back. When he got to the five-mile post, he looked down into the bucket and saw that the bottom had dropped out. Then he realized that he had heard something fall when he filled the bucket again, so he turned around and ran back to the spring and clapped in the bottom before the water had time to spill. The father thought that was a pretty quick trick, but the second man said, "Wait a minute. Give me a hoe, an axe and a plow." After he received the farm tools, he went out to ten acres of wood next to the house. Lickety-split he cut the trees, pulled the roots and rocks, ploughed the field, planted it in cow-peas (black-eyed peas) and had them cooked and seasoned for dinner. The father said, "Now that's a quick trick. Can't nobody beat that, and there is no use in trying!" He won the girl. But the last man said, "Just wait a minute!" He took his high-powered rifle and went out into the woods about seven or eight miles until "he spied a deer." He took aim and fired. Then he ran home, ran behind the house and set his gun down and then ran back out in the woods and caught the deer and held him until the bullet hit him. He won the girl.[94]

There is evidence that Hurston had her own love affair with beans. In a May 1936 letter, she writes, "My work is coming on most satisfactorily and I feel fine. I get up before sunrise and work on a tiny garden" where I am growing "peas (black-eye)…pole beans, [and] lima beans" despite there being a "terrible drought" here.[95] In July of the same year, she wrote:

My garden is in full swing. I got a full hamper of peas today and there is another hamper on the vines. I shall get somebody to take them to town and sell them for me since it is obvious that I cannot eat them all. I wonder if you would care to try some. Nothing would give me more pleasure than to send you something I raised. But if your cook does not know how to cook them it would be of no use. Still, I can send a recipe.[96]

Their Eyes Were Watching God concludes in the Florida Everglades, or the "muck," as Hurston calls the region. The muck is an agro-export plantation enclave populated with "hordes" of migrant workers who came in "truck loads close from east, west, north and south" to make money picking beans. While Tea Cake worked harvesting beans, Janie "baked big pans of navy beans with plenty of sugar and hunks of fatback laying on top...and boiled pots of black-eyed peas and rice," writes Hurston.[97]

Greens

Today, any native-born southerner, white or black, is a beans-and-greens-eating, corn-bread-pot-liquor-sopping person. If you are a northerner without southern roots, that last sentence likely puzzled you. Greens, a variety of leafy vegetables, have a long association with people of African descent in the U.S. South (and, by extension, the white folks around them). In eighteenth-century Africa, female toddlers of commoners accompanied their female elders into the forest to gather vitamin-rich "bush greens," different varieties of kale, collards and mustard greens to supplement what the men of their compounds produced and hunted. Over time, they domesticated these wild greens and learned to prepare them raw or cooked and seasoned them with salt, pepper, onions, garlic, herbs and pieces of meat and fish when they had access to them. Both Igbo women in southeastern Nigeria and Mande women across West Africa commonly served greens with chicken battered and deep fried in palm oil.[98] Enslaved and free blacks cultivated various types of leafy greens, including turnip, kale, callaloo (a spinach-like green) and collards, in subsistence gardens throughout the Americas.

The collard green plant comes from England, but black cooks in the South traditionally seasoned them in a distinctively West and Central African style. Black cooks learned how to season food using oral tradition and a prolonged apprenticeship in which people tasted each other's food and inquired what ingredients and cooking techniques they used. It was during these informal kitchen conversations that women exchanged family recipes for cooking collard greens and other garden bounty. Some of the secrets were as simple

Mrs. John L. Bishop with a girl in a collards garden, Aucilla, Florida, 1938. *Courtesy of State Archives of Florida, Florida Memory.*

as the use of a seemingly unlikely seasoning or marinade. Salt and pepper, crushed red pepper, bay leaf, sage and sugar are partly responsible for the down-home flavor associated with southern collard greens. Historically, black Floridian seasonings also made use of several fresh vegetables, including chopped scallions, onions or garlic. Apple cider vinegar and hot sauce are other staples. But what's most southern about Floridian-cooked vegetables is the inclusion of pork flavor in dishes like collards, kale and turnip greens.[99]

In 1923, boiled "collard greens about a foot long" served as part of the rations at Florida turpentine camps like the ones where Hurston conducted fieldwork.[100] Hurston describes greens as a staple, but she also describes their symbolic use in colloquial expressions and songs. In *Their Eyes Were Watching God*, Hurston uses greens as a figurative expression, saying that a group of characters "have got that fresh, new taste about them like young mustard greens in the spring."[101] Greens appeared in the folk rhymes and songs that Hurston collected in Florida. One went like this: "Some love collards/some love kale/I love a girl with a short shirt tail."[102]

Both elite blacks like Hurston and working-class blacks viewed well-seasoned greens as a delicacy. In *Seraph on the Suwanee*, the character Cup-

Cake rinsed "out a big pot, dropped a ham hock in it, and put it on the fire" to cook some greens. "He brought out the big bundle of turnip greens from the ice box and began to pick them over." Well-seasoned greens are described as so good that they could cure a sick man of whatever ailed him and make a dead man come alive. "Lay a good poultice of these, seasoned down with ham, against a man's ribs, and it'll just about cure him of whatever might ail him. Make a dead man set up on the cooling-board."[103]

Hurston recalls daydreaming about "turnip greens and dumplings" as men she had no interest in flirted with her. Speaking of love and romance, she goes on to say, "Under the spell of moonlight, music, flowers, or the cut and smell of good tweeds, I sometimes feel the divine urge for an hour, a day, or maybe a week. Then it is gone and my interest returns to corn pone and mustard greens."[104]

Greens were also a special-occasion food. Hoppin' John, collard greens and dumplings are popular New Year's Day dishes among Floridians. Black-eyed peas were believed to represent coins and the greens dollars that, if eaten, would bring economic prosperity for the New Year. In other parts of the world, folks have traditionally eaten lentils on New Year's with a similar rationale.[105]

Corn Dumplings Recipe
Makes about 20 dumplings

1 cup organic cornmeal, white or yellow, fine or medium
1 tablespoon all-purpose flour
½ teaspoon baking powder
¼ teaspoon salt
¼ teaspoon ground black pepper
1 cup hot potlicker from cooked greens
1 large egg, lightly beaten
¼ cup chopped scallions or onions, optional
2 vegetable bouillon cubes
6 pieces vegan or pork bacon, chopped
10 cups water

Mix the cornmeal, flour, baking powder, salt and pepper in a bowl. Stir in potlicker, a little at a time, to make smooth batter that is stiff enough to hold together. Vigorously stir in the egg, then fold in the scallions or onions. Let the batter rest for a few minutes. In a pressure cooker, add the bouillon, chopped bacon and water. Cover and simmer for about 30 minutes. You should have about 8 cups of stock. Drop the batter by the teaspoonful into the simmering stock. Cover the pot and cook until the dumplings are firm and cooked through, about 12 to 15 minutes. Serve with greens and hot sauce.[106]

YAMS AND SWEET POTATOES

The Portuguese introduced the South American plants cassava and sweet potatoes to Africa after the 1470s when they established trading posts on the west coast of Africa and in their colonies in Brazil. West and Central Africans used them like yams. In the equatorial forest regions of West and Central Africa, yams were such an important staple that some nicknamed it the "Yam Belt." Similar to plantains and cassava, African cooks steamed, boiled, grilled and fried yams and made them into flour for breads and fritters, fried chips and as fufu (also spelled foo foo), where the yams are boiled and pounded into a doughy consistency and then used like bread to eat with soups and stews. Fufu was and is particularly popular among the Ibo and Hausa of West Africa.[107]

Enslaved African women introduced yams to the Americas. Spanish slaveholders in Florida and the Caribbean learned they made better rations (along with the American sweet potato) than white or Irish potatoes because they did not spoil as fast. Enslaved Africans also cultivated sweet potatoes and yams in their subsistence gardens. By the mid-nineteenth century, African American slaves in many parts of the South had influenced whites to eat the tubers the same way they did.[108]

Hurston uses sweet potatoes to provide insight into gendered roles at public food events. In *Their Eyes Were Watching God*, bossy mayor Joe Starks instructs the men during a barbecue to "tell yo' womenfolks tuh do 'round 'bout some pies and cakes and sweet tater pone [or pudding]." The narrator goes on to say, "That's the way it went too. The women got together the sweets and the men looked after the meats." This gender division has an old history that began in the antebellum South. It's still noticeable at church events where the women prepare side dishes and desserts and the men barbecue meat and fry fish.[109]

County agent J.S. Johns in a sweet potato field in Baker County, 1929. *Courtesy of State Archives of Florida, Florida Memory.*

Sweet potatoes banked for storage, 1908. *Courtesy of State Archives of Florida, Florida Memory.*

Years later, Hurston recorded folk tales in the Florida Everglades about a giant sweet potato, illustrating the pride some had for family, region and potato pone:

> *They raises big vegetables down around the Everglades, too. Yes sir! That's rich land around down there. Take for instance, my old man planted sweet potatoes one year and when it come time to dig them potatoes, one of them had done got so big till they had to make a saw-mill job out of it. Well, they built a saw-mill and put whole crews of mens to work cutting up that big old sweet potato. And so that year everybody in Florida had houses made out of sweet potato slabs. And what you reckon everybody ate that year? Well, they lived off of potato pone, made out of the sawdust from that great big old tater my old man raised.*[110]

Another folklore Hurston collected describes Diddy-Wah-Diddy as "the largest and best-known of the Negro mythical places." It is a place where delicious cooked food is in abundance and free, including a big deep-dish sweet potato pie. According to Hurston, in Diddy-Wah-Diddy, the "pie is pushing and shoving to get in front of the traveler with a knife all stuck up in

People posing with a 36.5-pound sweet potato in St. Cloud, Florida, circa 1910. *Courtesy of State Archives of Florida, Florida Memory.*

the middle of it so he just cuts a piece off of that and so on until he finishes his snack. Nobody can ever eat it all up. No matter how much you eat it grows just that much faster."[111]

In her own work, Hurston's working-class characters consume sweet potatoes and yams interchangeably. For example, in *Seraph on the Suwanee*, there is one scene in which the staple appears in a sweet form as dessert and in side dishes such as a pudding, pone and French fries. "Towards sundown, she took the fryer out of the ice-box that Jim had killed for her the day before, and put it on the stove to fry, and mixed up a mess of soda biscuits." Hurston goes on to say, "She couldn't think of much to do, so she took some cold boiled sweet potatoes left over from the night before and sliced them and fried them brown in some bacon grease. Everything was already then."[112] In the same novel, Hurston also has her characters eating "baked yam."[113]

Sweet Potato Biscuits Recipe
Makes 12–15 small biscuits

1 cup sifted all-purpose flour
3 teaspoons baking powder
½ teaspoon salt
⅓ cup mashed sweet potatoes
About 3 tablespoons milk

Sift together dry ingredients. Cut in fat with two knives or a pastry blender. Add sweet potatoes and enough milk to make soft dough. Knead lightly, if desired. Roll to ½ inch thickness, cut in rounds, and place on a baking sheet. Bake in a hot oven (425° F) 15 to 20 minutes.[114]

Sweet Potato Chips Recipe

Sweet potatoes
Salt

Cut into thin slices, and steam until nearly done, the amount of sweet potatoes desired. Allow the surplus water to drain off between napkins. Fry in deep fat to a light brown. A little salt adds to its flavor.[115]

Sweet Potato Bread Recipe

1 cup finely mashed sweet potatoes
1 tablespoon warm water
½ yeast cake
1 teaspoon salt
1¾ cups flour, or sufficient to make soft dough

Add the salt to the potatoes, and the yeast; put in the water and flour enough to make a smooth sponge (about a cupful); cover, and set in a warm place to rise. When light, add the remainder of the flour or whatever is needed to make smooth, elastic dough. Cover and let rise until light; mould; shape into loaves or rolls; let rise and bake. Many variations of the above bread can be made by adding sugar, butter, lard, nuts, and spices.[116]

A 1936 letter indicates that Hurston had mastered the art of making a good sweet potato pudding. It was so good that she gave one away as an apology for a misunderstanding. In a letter to journalist, book columnist and literary editor Herschel Brickell, she writes, "So I'm grating some sweet potatoes right now to make you a nice potato pudding (tater pone, to you) because now I realize at last that you were just trying to give me some publicity."[117]

Sweet Potato Pone Recipe

2½ cups raw grated sweet potatoes (yams)
1 cup molasses
2 eggs
2 cups rich milk
1 tablespoon melted butter
1 teaspoon ground ginger or grated orange rind
1 tablespoon brown sugar
½ teaspoon powdered cinnamon

Mix ingredients and turn into a well-greased baking pan and bake about 45 minutes in a moderated oven, sprinkling the brown sugar and cinnamon over the top at the end of the first 25 minutes.[118]

Scalloped Sweet Potatoes with Apples Recipe

Sliced cooked sweet potatoes
Sliced raw apples
Sugar
Butter

Add just enough hot water to cover bottom of dish; the apples and sweet potatoes do not take up liquid. Bake covered in a moderately hot oven (375° F) 30 to 40 minutes or until apples are tender. If desired, uncover the dish, and top with crushed dry breakfast cereal or bread crumbs mixed with a little fat.[119]

Sweet Potato Cake Recipe

½ cup fat
1 cup sugar
2 eggs
1 cup mashed sweet potatoes
2 cups all-purpose flour
½ teaspoon salt
2 teaspoons baking powder
¼ teaspoon soda
½ teaspoon cinnamon
½ teaspoon nutmeg
¼ teaspoon cloves
½ cup milk
½ cup chopped nuts

To make, first cream the fat. Then add sugar gradually and cream well. Add eggs, beating well after each. Add sweet potatoes. Mix well. Sift together rest of the dry ingredients, and add alternately with milk to the creamed mixture, beginning and ending with the dry ingredients. Add nuts. Mix. Bake in a greased 9 x 9 x 2-inch loaf pan in a moderate oven (350° F) for 45 to 50 minutes. Top with caramel icing if desired.[120]

Chapter 3

FOLK MEDICINE RECIPES

Zora Neale Hurston's writings reveal an interest in natural prescriptions for the health challenges suffered by camp workers and plantation laborers. She also talks a great deal about natural remedies for poisoning. She incorporated what she learned about poisoning and natural remedies into her novel *Their Eyes Were Watching God* and other writings. Hurston writes, "Folk medicine is practiced by a great number of persons [in] sawmill camps, the turpentine stills, mining camps and among the lowly generally," who do not depend on conventional doctors to cure their ailments. Her subjects had more access to plant-based medicines, or what Hurston called the "folk medicine" and "primitive medicines," than modern medicine and doctors.[121] Those who did not and, because of lack of access, could not depend on conventional doctors were forced to learn how to safely use herbs that they could grow or forage and therefore were of no cost to them. The more they were forced to depend on these, the more they learned how to use them—for example, how much of the plant, which part of the plant and for what purpose. Once they learned how to use them properly, there was less risk of poisoning or hurting oneself, and this knowledge could be passed on for generations.

In her writings, Hurston recorded some food-based prescriptions for illnesses. How she collected and compiled the prescriptions is unknown. A study with empirical trials of their value is needed. Plants can contain toxins and carcinogens, and even universally eaten food plants such as peanuts can kill people who are allergic to them.[122]

Here are some prescriptions Hurston gathered in Florida and elsewhere. Where they came from specifically is unclear. A look at the ingredients in the natural prescriptions that Hurston records in her writings provides interesting insights into the history of folk medicine and food history. Nicole Farmer, MD, a board-certified internal medicine physician and a fellow at the Arizona Center for Integrative Medicine at the University of Arizona, says when "you think you are at your lowest, you learn how to utilize what is around you." Rural people of African descent are acculturated to "trust folk medicine," which is why so many of them "seek health counsel easily from… community members."[123]

STOMACH TROUBLES

Zora Neale Hurston's writings show an interest in finding a natural remedy for her stomach problems. Just like the people she researched, Hurston herself turned to plant-based remedies because race- and class-based modern medicine remained largely inaccessible or unequal for many rural Americans, black or white. Writing in 1931, Hurston says, "I continue to have

Payday for vegetable workers near Homestead, Florida, 1939. *Courtesy of Library of Congress.*

intestinal trouble but I keep it to myself. I really need medical attention...It slows me up and when I don't keep up the agar-agar I lose ground. Recently I just couldn't find the money for it, and it hasn't been so good."[124]

Agar agar, or simply agar, is a jelling agent native to Asia that is extracted from a type of red algae. People have used agar for decades as a natural remedy that aids the digestion process by lubricating the intestinal lining. Hurston probably used agar to relieve her stomach pains.[125] Her benefactor, Charlotte Osgood Mason, supplied Hurston with agar, one time sending a pound of it to her in the mail. When Hurston's stomach problems grew worse, Mason suggested that Hurston allow a white specialist to treat her at Mason's expense. Racist members of the physician's staff had Hurston wait in a closet filled with soiled laundry before the doctor examined her. It appears that the doctor did not find an antidote for her stomach problems because Hurston mentioned them thereafter. In a letter dated 1943 to Dr. Edwin Osgood Grover of Daytona Beach, Florida, she writes about being served a lunch in Sanford, Florida, that included pork chops, which "I could not refuse to eat them and thus offend my hostess. But pork" upset her stomach.[126]

Hurston's writings include references to other natural stomach remedies.

Upset Stomach Remedy Recipe
Makes 1 serving

Parched rice
Bay leaves
1 cup hot water

Make a tea of parched rice and bay leaves (6). Give a cup at a time. Drink no other water.[127]

Parched rice is made by stirring dry rice in a gas-heated tumbler or over an open fire for several hours. When the rice becomes very hot, it begins to expand as the rice germ is destroyed. At this point, the seed may not sprout, and the rice gains long-term storage capabilities.[128] Parched rice is a common food in many countries, notably Japan and India, where it is used to treat diarrhea and vomiting. In large doses, bay leaves induce vomiting, forcing the removal of what is causing the pain.[129]

Hurston also provides a prescription for what she describes as "Live Things in Stomach (Fits)" that seems to refers to people with stomach problems like those she suffered.

Live Things in Stomach (Fits) Remedy Recipe

½ cup sweet milk
Fresh garlic
Silver quarter with a woman's head on it

Take a silver quarter with a woman's head on it. Stand her on her head and file it in one-half cup of sweet milk. Add nine parts of garlic. Boil and give to drink after straining.[130]

Sweet milk is a term used to describe fresh, whole milk that is not cultured. The silver coin in garlic milk remedy would have worked to "delay the milk from turning sour for a few days more than usual," says Dr. Farmer. Milk is "often used as an immediate acid reducer," but over time, it does increase the stomach's acid level. Garlic is a remedy for acid reflux and heartburn. Garlic is also an "antibacterial agent against the bacteria responsible for peptic ulcers and dyspepsia symptoms like acid burning and indigestion," explains Dr. Farmer. Crushing garlic releases a variety of compounds, including one that acts as an antibiotic.

Based on her symptoms and the remedies she used, Dr. Farmer believes that Hurston most likely suffered from "bloating issues and gallbladder problems. Since dyspepsia symptoms showcase with gallbladder disease, the garlic milk remedy would still be effective." In the course of writing a scientific article regarding how cooking methods may alter phytochemicals in commonly used vegetables, Dr. Farmer researched phytochemicals in garlic, onions and other allium species. She says, "It seems that the saponin phytochemicals natural antibiotics in garlic have anti-spasm qualities. The saponins are actually very chemically stable, even in heated conditions, and I would think that, thus, a warm garlic milk remedy would have been very helpful."[131]

She adds that if Hurston "had issues with lactose intolerance or irritable bowel syndrome, then the milk and garlic would have irritated these ailments, respectively." The antimicrobial action of silver in milk would have prevented the growth of Lactobacillus species, which normally lower the lactose amount in milk. Perhaps Hurston "used the silver for its antimicrobial action and more than likely suffered from issues related to acid reflux or dyspepsia."[132]

THE CULT OF POISONING

The "cult of poisoning" exists "in fragmentary form from Africa" throughout the African diaspora, says Hurston. It "has built up an alertness and caution that is extreme in" some places. "In the United States, great masses of young Negro children are taught to eat and drink nowhere except at home. There is the gravest suspicion of unsolicited foods," Hurston observed.

"In most cases, it is a vegetable poison which makes them harder to detect than the mineral poisons so often used by the Europeans," says Hurston. Africans in the New World discovered poisonous and medicinal "plants and the most efficient use of them." Enslaved Africans also disembarked in the Americas with food farmacy (food as medicine) experts among them.[133]

Africans in colonial America, and in many instances for many years thereafter, represented a group versed in botany and experienced with plant poisons and herbal remedies. Plants taken in the wrong way or in the wrong amount could be harmful, if not fatal. A plant may have medicinal properties within its roots, oils and/or bark when used either internally or externally. Which part of the plant is used, how much and where it is applied are important factors, as one plant can have both medicinal and toxic properties.[134]

The theme of black paranoia and poisoning is illustrated in *Their Eyes Were Watching God*. When Janie and her husband, Joe Starks, grew estranged, Joe became convinced that Janie was poisoning his food. He sought an antidote from a black Floridian "root-doctor" from Altamonte Springs who began keeping close company with Joe, apparently treating him for poisoning. Janie feared that Joe had become dependent on the root doctor, whom she viewed as a scoundrel and fraud. Janie wanted her husband to use modern medicine, but he refused. Scared that his wife wanted to poison him and watch him die slowly, Joe Starks also turned to "old lady Davis to cook for him." Janie resented that her husband had more confidence in another woman's food, particularly someone she cooked better than and someone whose filthy kitchen might poison and kill Joe. "So [Janie] bought a beef-bone and made him some soup" to nurse Joe back to health. Joe refused to eat it, saying, 'Naw, thank you...Ah'm havin' uh hard enough time tuh try and git well as it is."[135] Hurt, Janie confided to her friend, saying, "Tuh think Ah been wid Jody twenty yeahs and Ah just now got tuh bear de name uh poisonin' him!"[136] Joe Starks "refused to admit her to his sick room" or eat the food she cooked. "This one and that one came to her house with covered plates of broth and other sick room dishes without taking the least notice of her as Joe's wife."[137] Hurston provides an antidote for poisoning that she calls "Medicine to Purge."[138]

Poisoning Antidote Recipe
Makes 1 serving

Jack of War tea
Pinch of soda (baking soda–sodium bicarbonate)
1 cup water

Jack of War tea and one tablespoon to a cup of water with a pinch of soda after it is ready to drink.[139]

No reliable sources could be found on Jack of War tea or soda and/or baking soda (sodium bicarbonate).

IN THE CAMPS, HOME-BASED MEDICINE

During her fieldwork, Hurston recorded other food-based antidotes for maladies commonly suffered among the working-class men and women she observed in Florida.[140] A look at natural prescriptions provides a rich history into folk medicines passed down from one generation to another through oral histories. They are also an indication of the agency that working people employed when confronted with daily hardships and suffering.

In Florida, operators of sawmill and turpentine camps and plantations depended on laborers trapped in debt peonage as their workforce. Lumber and turpentine represented "almost the only industries in the far-flung recesses of piney woods," according to a 1929 article in the *Chicago Defender*,

Gabriel Brown playing guitar, Eatonville, Florida, 1935. *Courtesy of State Archives of Florida, Florida Memory.*

an African American newspaper. In Florida, "the belt runs, roughly, from the counties about seventy-five miles south of Jacksonville, north and west along the gulf coast, out beyond Tallahassee, the capital. One of the largest of the naval stores [turpentine businesses] had 2,500 black laborers in different work camps scattered about...in several counties."[141]

> *Sound Recording 2*
> *A "shack-rouster" is a person responsible for waking up the workers in a labor camp. In this 1939 recording, Hurston sings a shack-rouster song she collected from a sawmill camp in Loughman, Polk County, Florida. June 1939, Florida Folklife, WPA Collections, Library of Congress, memory. loc.gov/cgi-bin/query/D?flwpabib:19:./temp/~ammem_qbNa*
>
> *Zora Neale Hurston, "Wake Up, Jacob" [Listen Now 1 min 34 sec]: memory.loc.gov/afc/afcflwpa/314/3144b1.mp3*

Turpentine camps in Taylor County, Florida, had a reputation for, as one worker put it, "Maybe you gits paid, an' maybe you don't. But if you run away an' they ketch you—wham! On the [chain] gang for six months."[142] It is unclear where she gained the prescriptions or at times the amount of each ingredient used in a recipe, but Hurston's writings provide all kinds of plant-related antidotes for injuries these workers suffered.

Anti-Inflammatory Recipe
Makes 1 serving

White rose oil
Lavender oil
Jockey club
Japanese honeysuckle

Combine together and rub on the swollen area.[143]

Hurston may have been referring to White Mountain Rose Oils, which comes from the *Cinnamomum camphora* (Lauraceae) plant. This plant produces several oils (white, brown and blue). The oil is a folk remedy for treating inflammations and as a weak antiseptic.[144] Lavender comes from the *Lavandula angustifolia* (English lavender) plant. Lavender is a folk remedy for sores, spasms, sprains and aches. In large doses, it becomes a narcotic poison.[145] Jockey club (shell-flower or *Alpinia zerumbet*), also commonly called boca de dragon, palo santo, shell ginger and tous maux, is in the ginger family. It is native to Asia and has flourished in Florida. Japanese honeysuckle (*Lonicera japonica*) is the common name of one of the many

Advertising for an herb seller, Belle Glade, Florida, 1937. *Courtesy of Library of Congress.*

different types of honeysuckle species. It has natural anti-inflammatory properties that reduce swelling and sores and is also an antibiotic.[146]

Sexually transmitted diseases were a problem in the camps and on the plantations. In her discussion of folk medicine, Hurston records one for gonorrhea.

Gonorrhea Remedy Recipe
Makes 1 serving

Handful of may pop roots (or passionflower)
One pint ribbon cane syrup
One-half plug of Brown's Mule tobacco cut up
Fifty cents of iodide potash

Take together three times a day as a tonic.[147]

No reliable sources could be found on the medicinal uses of maypop (passionflower, scientifically named *Passiflora incarnate*), a vine with a purple flower and green seeds that make a "pop" sound when stepped on. It has grown in Florida.[148] Ribbon cane has bands or ribbons around its stalk. Cultivated in the southern United States, it held the majority share of the commercial sugar industry until the 1960s. Like hog-killing season, communities had syrup time during which everyone pitched in to produce a sweet result. Ribbon cane stalks became a popular snack used like chewing gum and sold in country stores. People also used it as a sweetener at the breakfast table. It makes a darker cane syrup than regular sugar cane but not as dark as molasses. The darker the sugar, the more nutrient-rich it is. For example, clear sugar cane syrup has no redeeming nutritional qualities. In contrast, black strap molasses is rich in minerals and vitamins. Molasses is also high in calcium that removes toxins from the colon, manganese that is essential to the healthy functioning of the nervous system and potassium that assists in proper muscle contraction and nerve transmission. Molasses is also rich in vitamins B-1, B-2, B-6 and E. [149]

Tobacco was first grown and used by Native Americans for its pleasurable effects and for curing illnesses. Tobacco leaves, whole and in powdered form, were used to heal wounds and burns. In 1602, an anonymous doctor in

Zora Neale Hurston, 1935. *Courtesy of Library of Congress.*

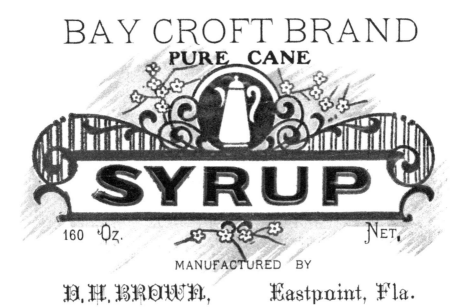

A label for Bay Croft Brand cane syrup company of East Point, Florida, circa 1900. *Courtesy of State Archives of Florida, Florida Memory.*

England argued that tobacco dried up gonorrhea by producing a discharge that rid the body of the disease. However, tobacco left too long on male genitalia could affect sperm production and cause male infertility.[150] As late as the 1920s, people made a salve out of burned tobacco leaves and lard to treat skin ulcers and gonorrhea lesions.[151]

Potash (potassium carbonate) is called *kanwa* or *akanwu* in contemporary Nigeria. The word comes from the process of leaching and evaporating plant and wood ashes in large iron pots, thus the name potash. West Africans used it to tenderize, emulsify and preserve food. It's also used in beer brewing and baking. Germans use it like baking soda to make gingerbread. Potash has a number of medicinal qualities. It is used for toothache relief, as a stomach antacid and for relief of constipation and flatulence. It's been proven effective in treating inflammatory bowel disease. In the correct doses, potash is a liver stimulant. It increases urination and enhances renal blood flow. In the respiratory system, potash acts as an expectorant that clears mucous congestion.[152] Users must exercise caution, however, as in large doses potash is poisonous and can cause sometimes fatal damage to the stomach and esophagus.[153]

CURES FOR THE AILING MIND

In the last section of the novel *Their Eyes Were Watching God*, a large rabies-infected dog bites Tea Cake, leaving him mentally disturbed. Over time, Tea Cake turns on his wife, Janie, just like the ferocious mad dog. "All he needed was for the doctor to come on with that medicine," says Janie.[154] But the medicine necessary to cure him was far away from the rural Everglades in the city of Palm Beach. Tea Cake's demise also hints at the perceived link between mysticism and illness. When Tea Cake's friend and co-worker Sop tells him that a man whom Tea Cake was jealous of had returned to the muck, the assumption became that it was "mysterious" that he took sick the same time that his rival reappeared. "People didn't just take sick like this for nothing."[155]

During her fieldwork, Hurston recorded an antidote for what she describes as "Loss of Mind."

Loss of Mind Remedy Recipe
Makes 1 serving

Sheep weed leaves
Bay leaf
Fig leaf
Poison oak
Sarsaparilla root
2 cups of water

Take the bark and cut it all up fine. Make a tea. Take one tablespoon and put in two cups of water and strain and sweeten. You drink some and give some to patient. Put a fig leaf and poison oak in shoe. (Get fig leaves off a tree that hasn't borne fruit. Stem them so that nobody will know.)[156]

Folk remedies were based not only on natural cures but a little bit of mysticism, too. That philosophy existed among natural remedy practitioners in Florida. Sheep weed leaves (*Rumex acetosella*), also known as sheep's sorrel, sour weed and red sorrel, is a variety of sorrel weed with arrow-shaped leaves and maroon flowers. The leaves, juice and roots are known to be anti-inflammatory and antibacterial, as well as a diuretic, antioxidant and laxative.[157] Bay leaves were once employed to treat hysteria. Sarsaparilla root (*Smilax regelii* and *Smilax aspera*), an antioxidant, is native to Central America and known for its use in soft drinks.[158] Fig leaves are rich in fiber and calcium and beneficial for improving sleep and energizing the body. They are also a laxative.[159] Poison oak (*Toxicodendron diversilobum* and *Toxicodendron pubescens*) is a shrub or vine, depending on the species. It ranks among the more painful of plants to humans and results in a rash and severe swelling upon skin contact. However, poison oak has also been found to treat muscle stiffness and arthritis. The juice of poison oak, when taken in very small doses, may work as a sedative.[160]

FEMALE-SPECIFIC REMEDIES

Women also worked in the turpentine camps and suffered their own hardships. Camp officials mistreated female the same as male workers. Men and women slept in the same barracks on the plantation with no provision made to separate them.[161] Hurston describes an antidote for curing what she calls "flooding," or excessive menstrual bleeding. (There is no indication that Hurston suffered from a similar challenge.)[162]

Excessive Menstrual Bleeding Remedy Recipe
Makes 1 serving

Grated nutmeg
Pinch of alum
Quart of boiling water

One grated nutmeg, pinch of alum in a quart of water (cooked). Take one-half glass three times daily.[163]

The Chinese used powdered nutmeg seeds for menstrual cramps because it is an astringent and relieves gas.[164] "According to Chinese medicine," says

Dr. Farmer, "nutmeg is a warming spice that helps women" who have "an imbalance in the spleen-pancreas pathway" that causes excessive bleeding, weakness and cold body temperatures. "Nutmeg also helps to inhibit prostaglandin, a hormone-like molecule that is responsible for causing inflammation, painful menstrual cycles and relaxes the smooth muscle in the uterus."[165] Alum is a type of compound. There are several forms of alum, but potassium alum (potash alum) is the most common form. Its medicinal properties include the ability to reduce bleeding.[166]

CONCLUSION

How effective or ineffective the natural remedies Hurston recorded were is unclear. There is no indication that she stayed around long enough to observe an application and treatment over time. Instead, Hurston provides a cataloging of recipes and anecdotes on when and how people used them. However, that information is not enough to come to treatment conclusions regarding effectiveness. Neither do I have the training to evaluate the natural remedies she records. The question of the effectiveness of natural remedies with rising costs of healthcare, high unemployment rates and high numbers of people without medical insurance is an important one. Perhaps we will see the growing sector of underinsured people today turning to natural remedies like they did among the working poor Hurston studied in Florida.

Chapter 4

FIVE HELPIN'S OF CHICKEN

C hicken was not a foreign food to slaves brought to Florida. In the pre-colonial period, the Yoruba, Akan and other ethnic groups in West and Central Africa fried, roasted, barbecued and stewed fowl. It was not the food of the common people, however.[167] Most did not eat chickens because they had to "either belong to the nobility or have the means to buy such items," wrote the Dutch traveler Pieter de Marees in 1602.[168] Chicken was reserved for special occasions. In preparation for a funeral, de Marees goes on to say, people cooked "fowls and other food which they usually eat."[169]

One found chicken used in West and Central African stews and gumbos. In a letter written around 1788, a traveler tell us that on the Ivory Coast "the diet of the poorest sort included rice, fish, fowl, kid, and elephants' flesh, and all this boiled and thickened with palm oil and a vegetable substance called ocra [*sic*]."[170] Prolific slaver Theodore Canot says in the 1850s that the Baga people made stews with "tender fowls smothered in snowy rice."[171] The Baga people live in Guinea Bissau and its immediate surrounding area. This is the region where Canot did a lot of trading.

Jerking, barbecuing, grilling and frying chicken are cooking techniques that Africans practiced before arriving in the Americas. They also used chicken in gumbo and jambalaya-like stews made with okra.[172] In the West African Gold Kingdom of Guinea, common women ran local village markets in the 1600s and thereafter. They would arrive daily after "walking five, some of them even six miles" to the market in groups of three or four usually singing "and greatly enjoy[ing] themselves on the road."[173] They came loaded down

Fried chicken and biscuits hot out of the oven, 1941. *Courtesy of Library of Congress.*

with children and food and traded their food for fish to carry home; they often returned home from the market as loaded as when they started. They arrived at the markets at sunrise carrying "chickens, eggs, bread, and such necessaries as people in the coastal towns need to buy," de Marees writes.[174] They set up their businesses on fixed market days "on which one finds more for sale there than on other days. If one Town has its great Market-day on one day, another Town has its Market on another day: thus they keep their Market-days on separate days," and all food markets remained closed on Sunday. Some sold small amounts of delicious-smelling and tasting chicken that they cooked on small portable stoves.[175]

Chickens were among the first contingent of passengers that arrived with Columbus on his second voyage in 1493. With few predators or diseases and left to feed freely on the rich grasses, roots and wild fruits, they reproduced quickly.[176] "There is some confusion about domesticated fowls. The turkey and Muscovy duck were certainly present in pre-Columbian America, and some think that a type of chicken was also," writes historian Alfred W. Crosby Jr. He adds, "Most of the chickens in America by 1600 were of European descent, plus a considerable number of guinea hens of African origin."[177]

EARLY AMERICA

During the antebellum period, southerners considered chicken "a semi-luxury item," and elites had their slaves cook it frequently.[178] "The most notable dish was fried chicken," says historian Sam Bowers Hilliard. "But frying required a young bird, which was not always available. Those too old and tough for frying were roasted or boiled until tender, and leftover chicken or turkey carcasses were converted into pies with large dumplings made of wheat flour."[179]

Planters set small parcels of land aside for their slaves to raise chickens. What they did not use to supplement their rations they sold on Sunday, the traditional market day and a day off for slaves. Chickens were one of the items they raised in their gardens and sold in local markets.[180]

Butchers, street vendors and restaurant and tavern owners purchased enslaved Africans and employed free blacks to cook and serve food in their businesses. They also used enslaved Africans as laborers who their masters turned over to them to work as punishment, and they rented slaves, paying their owners in money or in food.[181] These black cooks helped make their owners and employers wealthy.

Historian Eugene Genovese writes that enslaved Africans in the Americas who had "a healthy concern with cooking" disseminated their fetish for fried chicken and other forms of chicken among the non-Africans they lived and worked around.[182] And blacks had a monopoly on the sale of fried chicken.[183] Like a lot of other street foods sold in slave societies, these chickens that had been raised in the African entrepreneurs' gardens were cooked and then sold on street carts the slaves made and rigged with portables stoves as they did in Africa. In heavily trafficked pedestrian sectors of urban centers, African American street vendors sold chicken parts such as wings, backs, gizzards and other organ meats for five cents and the better cuts of the bird for ten cents. Chicken weren't only a source of nutrition; they filled the pocketbook as well as the belly.[184]

African American entrepreneurs selling fried chicken played an important social role in urban cities like Jacksonville, Florida. African and African American newcomers commonly sought out street vendors who sold a taste of home and spoke their language. These entrepreneurs often set up their mobile eateries in the business districts that employed a large number of people, near public transportation stops and in neighborhood meeting places such as food markets. In these spaces, fried chicken vendors became a part of the urban landscape. Historically, many new arrivals turned to selling food as street vendors as one of their first forms of employment because it required little in the way of licenses, language skills or formal training. An enterprising fried chicken vendor could over time save enough money to open a brick-and-mortar restaurant, tavern or boardinghouse. Selling fried chicken created a chance to go into business for oneself and possibly purchase the freedom of loved ones who were still enslaved. For the street vendor, fried chicken prepared inexpensively and sold at a profit could provide an avenue to increased economic opportunity and freedom.

HURSTON'S WRITINGS AND EXPERIENCES

The late 1920s to the late 1930s served as Hurston's most productive writing years when she published *Color Struck*, a 1926 play; *Cold Keener*, a 1933 play; *Mules and Men*, a 1935 book; *Their Eyes Were Watching God*, a 1937 novel; and *Tell My Horse*, a 1938 book, just to name a few of her works during this period. Yet being prolific did not translate to financial gain, and she remained a struggling artist. And so as generations had before her, Hurston hatched a plan to use chicken as a way to generate income and raise her up from her current circumstance.

In a 1931 letter, Hurston pitched the concept of starting a food business specializing in all things chicken: chicken bouillon, chicken salad, chicken à la king, fried chicken and chicken soup.[185] Hurston had mastered the art of cooking chicken, and she knew it. She writes, "I like to cook" and was prepared to "write personal letters to some of the finer hostesses and try to establish myself as New York's Chicken Specialist."[186] "I'm an expert at cooking chicken," says Hurston, "and because I am an expert, it will not take me a long time to cook it, and I can make enough money cooking and selling chicken to give myself the economic independence and time needed to be a prolific author. I firmly believe that I shall succeed as a writer, but the time element is important."[187]

"I don't need any real capital to do it. A few glass jars made to my order for the soup. Perhaps a half dozen gallon thermos jugs in which to deliver hot fried chicken. Oiled paper-lined cartons for salad and à la king." Hurston expected to pay for the startup cost "by denying myself a few things for a short while."[188]

Her business development plan called for using word of mouth to obtain fifty to one hundred clients who would hire her to make chicken dishes specific to their needs and tastes. "I aim to make the soup so well that it can be served as cold consommé or hot as clear soup or used as stock by the client in her own kitchen," Hurston wrote. She goes on to say, "The breasts of chicken I would cut off before the chicken was put in the soup-pot. I'd steam these breasts almost without water and when thoroughly done, they'd be my salad material. The other part of the chicken would emerge as à la king. Then I'd have a certain amount of fresh chicken livers to dispose of also."[189] Hurston pitched the food business idea, but she never launched it. As a child, chicken had been an essential part of Hurston's African American table in Eatonville, Florida, where she raised chicken, ate chicken and learned how to cook chicken. "We had chicken on the table often," she writes.[190]

Chicken Fritters Recipe

2 cups chopped leftover chicken
4 tablespoons chopped green pepper
2 teaspoons baking powder
¼ teaspoon salt
2 eggs
4 tablespoons chopped parsley
1½ cups flour
1 cup thin cream
¼ teaspoon pepper
1 teaspoon melted butter

Mix and sift the dry ingredients.
Beat the eggs thoroughly, and add to the cream. Add the liquid mixture gradually to the dry mixture and beat until light. Add chicken, butter, pepper, and seasonings. Beat with rotary egg beater. Drop by spoonful in piping hot fat. Drain each fritter and serve hot with chicken gravy.[191]

Chicken Pancakes Recipe

1½ cups flour
3½ teaspoons baking powder
3 teaspoons sugar
1 teaspoon salt

1 egg, beaten lightly
¾ cup milk
3 tablespoons melted butter
¾ cup ground chicken
1 teaspoon minced onion
⅛ teaspoon pepper or less

Measure flour, baking powder, sugar, and salt into the sifter. Mix. Sift into a mixing bowl. Add milk and beaten egg; when well blended, add the melted shortening, ground chicken, minced onion, and pepper. Beat well. Fry like any pancake on a hot griddle until golden brown.[192]

Chicken Hash Recipe

1 (or more) fowl
Potatoes
Green peppers
Onions
Evaporated milk (large-size can)

Cut fowl for fricassee and cook in sufficient water to barely cover, preferably the day before using. One cup of white cooking wine can be substituted for one cup of water if desired. Celery tops and onion can be included in the boiling process. When tender, remove meat, strain stock and let cool. Cut meat into small cubes; put skin and gizzard through meat grinder. Peel enough potatoes to approximate, but not quite equal, the meat; cut meat in small cubes and parboil. Put ground-up chicken skin and fat from stock in large skillet over low flame. Slice two or three green peppers and an equal amount of onion (depending on size and taste) and simmer in chicken fat until well done, but not brown. Add stock if necessary to keep from burning. Add chicken and potatoes. Stir until warm, sprinkle with flour; continue stirring, add salt, pepper and celery seed to taste. Stir in one can evaporated milk and dilute with stock. Mixture should be creamy but not soupy. This dish takes time to prepare but can be made the day before and reheated when ready to use. [The original recipe called for heavy cream and butter.][193]

SPECIAL-OCCASION FOOD

Because Hurston's father was a pastor in Florida, "our house was a place where people came," she writes. "Visiting preachers, Sunday school, and B.Y.P.U. (Baptist Young Peoples Union) workers, and just friends. There was fried chicken for visitors, and other such hospitality as the house afforded."[194] Just as the Igbo, Hausa and Mande of West Africa all ate poultry on special occasions, cooking and serving fried chicken on special occasions was common to African Americans of every status.

In the novel *Their Eyes Were Watching God*, fried chicken is the central part of the wedding reception meal when Janie marries her first husband, Logan Killicks. They marry in her grandmother's parlor on a Saturday evening "with three cakes and big platters of fried rabbit and chicken." Later in the novel, Tea Cake celebrates winning a big pot from shooting dice in Jacksonville by giving a dinner party that night "free to all" with "a big table loaded down with fried chicken and biscuits and a wash-tub-full of macaroni with plenty of cheese in it," writes Hurston. One roustabout ruins the party by trying to "pull and haul over all the chickens and pick out the livers and gizzards to eat." Even after Tea Cake warns him to stop, the man "kept right on plowing through the pile uh chicken. So Tea Cake got mad," and the men fight over the fried chicken.[195]

In his book *The Souls of Black Folk* published in 1903, W.E.B. Du Bois tells of the time when he served as a teacher in a country school in rural Tennessee at the turn of the century. Upon receiving an invitation to eat at someone's home, he says, "I was often invited to 'take out and help' myself to fried chicken" biscuits, a side dish and dessert.[196] Hurston and her contemporaries, however, did express the opinion that fried chicken could become the special-occasion southern food that was so plentiful you could get sick of eating it. As Hurston recalls, in her childhood home, "we were never hungry," but "chicken and fish were too common with us."[197]

Like Hurston, writer James Weldon Johnson was a native Floridian. Johnson grew up in Jacksonville and attended the same boarding school as Hurston. He tells the story of working one summer as a teacher around the 1900s at a rural segregated school about thirty miles south of Atlanta. He rented a room as a boarder. "I was gratefully surprised by the fare my landlady set before me; the main course being fried chicken twice a day, for breakfast and supper. However, at the end of two or three weeks it appeared that I had eaten every chewable chicken on the place. At first, this was something of a relief, for I had made the astounding discovery that man cannot live by fried chicken alone."[198]

Jim Crow laws barred African Americans from segregated hotels. As a result, black researchers and intellectuals like Hurston remained dependent on boardinghouses and private hosts in private homes that most often served honored guests fried chicken. A series of lecture and/or fieldwork in the South would often leave one tired of eating fried chicken.

In the South during the Jim Crow era, a black person commonly ate fried chicken out of a shoebox while traveling. Mothers and grandmothers also packed fried chicken in baskets for Sunday picnics. In Hurston's play *Color Struck*, couples eat fried chicken out of a picnic basket. The stage direction in the script reads, "Everybody begins to open baskets. All have fried chicken… Delicacies are swapped from one basket to the other. John and Emma offer the man next to them some supper. He takes a chicken leg."[199]

Similarly, about 1891, James Weldon Johnson tells the story of his mother sending him off to college in Atlanta with a box lunch on a Jim Crow train from his hometown of Jacksonville. The box contained "fried chicken, slices

Mrs. McLelland cooking fried chicken for Sunday dinner in 1942, Escambia Farms, Florida. *Courtesy of Library of Congress.*

Signaling from a Jim Crow car in 1943, St. Augustine, Florida, 1943. *Library of Congress.*

of buttered bread, hard-boiled eggs, a little paper of salt and pepper, an orange or two, and a piece of cake." In those days, black folks on long train rides always traveled with shoebox lunches that included fried chicken, buttered bread and pound cake.

Blacks had to sit apart from white customers in eating cars or restaurants, and because of this, purchasing food in these spaces while traveling subjected nonwhites to harsh indignities. To get around this, African Americans did not simply capitulate but rather employed what political scientist James Scott calls "infrapolitics," or everyday forms of resistance.[200] Packing and eating a shoebox meal of fried chicken is a good example of this. Doing so allowed one to avoid the humiliation of ordering food at a "colored" window or seating area in a white-owned restaurant or cafeteria.

Fried Chicken Recipe

1 chicken
Flour
Salt
Pepper

Cut the chicken up, separating every joint, and wash clean. Salt
and pepper it, and roll into flour well. Have your fat very hot, and
drop the pieces into it, and let them cook brown. The chicken
is done when the fork passes easily into it. After the chicken is
all cooked, leave a little of the hot fat in the skillet; then take a
tablespoon of dry flour and brown it in the fat, stirring it around,
then pour water in and stir till the gravy is as thin as soup.[201]

A COURTING FOOD

Hurston's fieldwork also points to courting rituals using chicken. One sees
southern black men in Florida offering chicken as a way of indicating their
romantic interest. For example, while doing fieldwork in Woodbridge in
Orange County, Florida, Hurston attended a toe party. A group of women
would hide themselves behind a curtain with their toes sticking out. "Some
places you take off yo' shoes and some places you keep 'em on, but most all
de time you keep 'em on," explained one participant to Hurston. "When all
de toes is in a line, sticking out from behind de sheet they let de men folks
in and they looks over all de toes and buys de ones they want for a dime.
Then they got to treat de lady dat owns dat toe to everything she want." The
foods listed among the treats included chicken perleau and baked and fried
chicken.[202] The vittles at the party included pigs' feet and chitterlings.[203]

Chicken pilau is a traditional chicken and rice dish (also made in Florida
with shrimp or meat as the protein source). The word "pilau" derives from
the Persian word *pilav* or *pilaw*, which is also the origin of rice pilaf. The rice
and chicken combination has its roots in Middle Eastern and West Asian
cookery. Berber traders and travelers spread it across Africa, and enslaved
Africans introduced it to the Americas during the African slave trade. It
became especially common in Florida and other parts of the Americas.

Chicken pilau, bogs and Latin American *arroz con pollo* (rice with chicken) are cousins. Rice and chicken combinations cooked in Dutch ovens and cast-iron skillets have held global popularity for centuries because they are easy to cook and can feed large numbers of people.[204]

Chicken Pilau Recipe

1 chicken
Salt
Pepper
Rice
Eggs

Cut large fricassee chicken in pieces as for frying. Cover well with water and cook slowly until meat is tender. Add salt and pepper to taste. Most Southerners like a pilau highly peppered. Add washed uncooked rice. There should be three cups of liquid to every cup of uncooked rice. Cover, stir once, and cook over a low fire until rice is tender and has absorbed the liquid, about 20 or 25 minutes. Hard-boiled eggs are sometimes cut into pilau when done.[205]

In addition to live music and moonshine at these courting rituals, chicken pilau, grilled chicken and pan-fried chicken attracted large numbers of working-class men and women to rural outdoor parties.[206] At one of them, a male participant named Charlie Jones insisted that Hurston "have a treat on me!…You done ate chicken and ham with every shag-leg in Orange County *but* me. Come on and spend some of *my* money." Hurston replied, "Thanks, Charlie, but I got five helpin's of chicken inside already. I either got to get another stomach or quit eating."[207]

Continuing on the theme of courtship and marriage, Hurston shares insights about 1920s and 1930s black men's views on skin complexion and black women in a folklore involving the preferred woman cooking chicken for her man:

> *You marry a yaller or a brown woman and wake her up in de night and she will sort of stretch herself and say, "I know what I was dreaming when you woke me up. I was dreaming I had done baked you a chicken and cooked*

you a great big old cake, and we was at de table eating our dinner out of de same plate, and I was sitting on your lap and we was just enjoying ourselves to death!" Then she will kiss you more times than you ask her to, and go on back to sleep. But you take and wake up a black gal, now! First thing she been sleeping wid her fists balled up, and you shake her, she'll lam you five or six times before you can get her awake. Then when she do git wake she'll have off and ast you, "Nigger, what you wake me up for? Know what I was dreaming when you woke me up? I dreamt dat you shook your old rusty black fist under my nose and I split your head open wid a axe." Then she'll kick your feets away from hers, snatch de covers all over on her side, ball up her fists agin, and gwan back to sleep.[208]

This is such a coded, jarring and problematic food and passion passage. In collecting and sharing it, Hurston provides a mocking portrait of black male sexual and culinary desires during the 1920s to the 1940s and a glimpse into the kind of color coding and sexual politics that occurred in black communities and was described in African American literature.

The passage encrypts a gender and class dynamic among African Americans while translating them in the vocabulary of skin tone. According to the black male narrator, African American women exist on a spectrum from least desired to most desired in shades from coal black to high yellow. The lighter the complexion, the popular cultural theory in the black community says, the better able to meet a man's needs, chief among them good food— chicken and cake—sexual pleasure in bed and respect. In the passage, the "middle-class" norms of a polite society trickle up the color spectrum, but at the same time, economic realities don't allow poor lower-class black women the necessary resources, time and energy to prepare an elaborate chicken meal and provide sexual pleasure after eight or more hours of hard labor outside the home. The image of "the black gal's" fist and her man's "rusty black fist" signifies the hard physical labor both do in order to put food on the table and survive. Among the lower classes that Hurston studied, little time existed after long workdays for the preparation of food like baked chicken and cake except for special occasions. And fatigue from hard labor must have made time for tenderness on a work night hard to come by, too. In contrast, middle-class women married to African American entrepreneurs or professionals tended to be lighter in complexion than poor, dark-skinned women. Middle-class women had the ability to work in the home and employ a domestic servant to prepare dinner. Such women would have had more time and energy for the kind of treatment the narrator desires.

COMFORT FOOD

It's often during long times away from home that we dream about the foods we grew up with, even those that at times we became sick of eating. For southern migrants like Hurston, chicken—particularly fried chicken and chicken and dumplings—carried with it nostalgic memories of childhoods spent in the South.

In several of her writings, Hurston provides a view of chicken as a longed-for childhood comfort food. In a fantasy she had at Florida Baptist Academy in Jacksonville, she turns the table on a wealthy female rival classmate who holds her in contempt because she is poor. Hurston dreams of eating fried chicken in her palace while her rival suffers a terrible meal. "When I would be grown and sit up in my fine palace eating beef stew and fried chicken, that duty-girl was going to be out in my backyard gnawing door-knobs."[209] Hurston writes that poor African Americans dream about eating chickens, and those like the shiftless Eatonville resident Coon Taylor steal them from their neighbors' chicken coops when they cannot afford to buy them. But in a poor southerner's fantasy world, chickens are free and already cooked.[210] In the African American mystical fantasy city Diddy-Wah-Diddy, one could eat chicken to their heart's desire.

> *If a traveler* [in Diddy-Wah-Diddy] *gets hungry all he needs to do is to sit down on the curbstone and wait and soon he will hear something hollering "Eat me! Eat me! Eat me!" and a big baked chicken will come along with a knife and fork stuck in its sides. He can eat all he wants and let the chicken go and it will go on to the next one that needs something to eat. Nobody can ever eat it all up. No matter how much you eat it grows just that much faster. Everybody would live in Diddy-Wah-Diddy if it wasn't so hard to find and so hard to get to.*[211]

CONCLUSION

Historically, Floridians and other southerners loved fried chicken, considering it a comfort and special-occasion food. Blacks favored fried chicken because of their cultural heritage, taste preferences and long history of monopolizing the sale of it in the antebellum South as street vendors, caterers and the owners and operators of food service enterprises that served fried chicken.[212]

But chickens have been used to exploit racist stereotypes. During the antebellum period, southerners blamed the theft of chickens on enslaved African Americans. During Reconstruction and thereafter, anti-black sectors sought to create public doubt in black elected officials through exploitative images of dumb blacks stealing chickens. This racist propaganda was effective and helped to ease the whites' fears over free black men holding office in Florida and other parts of the South.[213] Psyche A. Williams-Forson has written about poultry and U.S. culture. She says, "In using a food object to project these cultural stereotypes, whites were able to capitalize on a known truth: that black people raised and sometimes ate chicken. Added to this was a gross oversimplification—black people were chicken stealers."[214]

For many Florida communities, chicken is a staple and an essential food at a reunion, graduation party, wedding, funeral, barbecue and a multitude of other special occasions. A cooked chicken's importance, as illustrated in the Diddy-Wah-Diddy fable, still rings true today among many Floridians and other southerners.

Today, younger generations are consuming high-fat, high-calorie fried chicken more frequently. Yet because they are far more sedentary than their ancestors, this affinity is not for the best. The transition from rural to urban folk who get less exercise than their descendants and fried chicken from a special-occasion food to a staple (combined with an increased consumption of sweet, salty and other fatty foods) finds southerners today with disproportionally high levels of obesity and risk factors for heart disease, high blood pressure and diabetes. During Hurston's time, Floridians lived in predominantly rural settings performing hard labor and getting lots of other physical activity. High in saturated fat, fried chicken gave them needed calories for doing hard labor, but it did contribute to poor health because fat clogs arteries. However, they ate fried chicken generally on special occasions, and they ate far less sweet, salty and fatty foods than today. Today's Floridians would do well to still enjoy their chicken but do it in more health-conscious ways.[215] For a light version of fried chicken, one southerner developed an interesting strategy. She takes skinless chicken parts, dips them in seasoned flour and then oven-bakes them with a little oil in a pan. After the chicken has browned, it is covered with aluminum foil and cooked for a few additional minutes.[216]

Chapter 5

I'LL MEET YOU AT
THE BARBECUE

For Zora Neale Hurston and those she studied in Florida, as financially needy people most of their lives, barbecues were a rarity. As one sees in this chapter, a whole barbecued hog was often at the center of large events during the summer months like a political campaign event, a holiday like the Fourth of July or other special occasions like a community celebration. It was also used as barter for workers who performed strenuous work. Today, health professionals tell us that the consequences of eating barbecued pork high in saturated fat on special occasions depends on one's health and eating and exercise patterns. Those who are already in poor health and have poor eating and exercise habits and eat barbecued pork on more than special occasions increase their risk factors for an aneurysm or heart attack.[217]

There is no doubt that Zora Neale Hurston loved barbecued pork. Cooking outdoors with fire was, in her words, a heavenly experience made complete by barbecued meats that were as blessed as manna from heaven. She writes, "Maybe all of us who do not have the good fortune to meet or meet again, in this world, will meet at a barbecue."[218] There was a white-owned large barbecue stand on Route 17 north of Jacksonville, Florida, called Diddy-Wah-Diddy. Hurston writes that the owner chose the name because he had heard African Americans in the area defining it as a "mythical place of good things to eat, especially the barbecue."[219] There is also John the Conquer, the "hope bringer" from an African American fable whose tales come from the antebellum period. Hurston recorded a story about John being bold enough to barbecue some of the devil's pigs over hell's burning fires. John and the

Devil "had some words" before John escaped to continue his search for "a song that would whip Old Massa's earlaps down."[220]

In Hurston's John the Conquer tale, John is the "pit master," "the master cook" or what one 1931 source calls "the chief cook" at the barbecue.[221] It is John who understands barbecue as a method of "turn[ing] the dampers down in old Original Hell" in order to barbecue "some of the Devil's hogs… over the coals."[222]

HISTORY

Florida barbecue has its roots in Native American, Spanish and African culinary heritage. The Arawak people of the Caribbean had a diet that included a lot of non-sauce barbecuing of meat on green wood grills they called *brabacots*. The Spanish translated the word to *barbacoa*, from which we get the English word barbecue.[223] The Spanish learned from Native Americans how to barbecue the pig and popularized the cooking style among European settlers in their colonies. They brought the barbecue culture they had learned in the Caribbean with them to Florida, which they held from 1736 to 1801.[224] Before their arrival in the Americas, West and Central Africans learned how to cook whatever wild game villagers brought home. Africans cooked most meats over an open pit and ate them with a sauce similar to what we now call a barbecue sauce made from lime or lemon juice and hot peppers.

Africans came from regions where they barbecued during feast days. As they disembarked at ports throughout colonial America, Africans spread their barbecue knowledge wherever they were brought. Today, Floridians are most associated with adding lime or lemon to their tomato-based barbecue sauce. Carolina pit barbecue seems closest to what we see with West and Central African barbecue with a heavy hand on hot peppers, lemon and/or lime.[225]

In historian Eugene Genovese's words, Africans in the antebellum South "contributed more to the diet of the poorer whites than the poorer whites ever had the chance to contribute to theirs."[226] In addition, the majority of white elites depended on African Americans to barbecue their meat. The former slave Louis Hughes recalls the popular view that "slaves could barbecue meats best, and when the whites had barbecues slaves always did the cooking."[227]

In a second John the Conqueror tale Hurston records, John shames a rural "trashy" poor white couple, ordering them to consume their "barbecue and likker" out back in the kitchen away from the honored guests attending his barbecue. In the story, the marginalized couple is restricted to a space where the hog is butchered and prepared for barbecuing. The privileged are given access to the prized spaces where the host distributes the best cuts of meat.[228]

Making the Pit

Hurston's writing and sources from the same period show that the method of barbecuing a whole hog has not changed in centuries. In the Eatonville community barbecue scene in the novel *Their Eyes Were Watching God*, "the day before the lightening, [Hambo and Pearson] dug a big hole in back of the store," writes Hurston.[229] A good barbecue pit should be "approximately ten feet long, nine feet wide, and three or four feet deep," according to a 1931 article on southern barbecue.[230] Similarly, other sources describe pit barbecue in the areas Hurston studied and from where immigrants came to those places as laborers. A Works Progress Administration record called for "digging…a pit some six feet long and possibly two feet deep."[231] A WPA account of a candidate's barbecue tells us that the day before the event, a group of men under the supervision of pit master "Dad Crummit [who] has

Barbecuing meat at a Masonic event in Kissimmee, Florida, 1886. *Courtesy of State Archives of Florida, Florida Memory.*

Cooking barbecue at a Tin Can Tourists convention, Arcadia, Florida, circa 1920. *Courtesy of State Archives of Florida, Florida Memory.*

presided over every barbecuing here for thirty years," dug a pit "three feet wide, three deep, and ten feet long."[232] It is unclear how the size or depth of the pit affects the cooking. The heat of the fire and the type of wood used seem more critical to the cooking.

MAKING CHARCOAL

Cooking over a pit fire is difficult because one has to keep the coals set at the ideal temperature for long hours. Southern pit masters burn down hardwood until they have a pit full of red-hot, glowing coals. The wood the pit master selects to make coals makes a difference in the taste of the meat. Some use "dry white oak and hickory for these produce a hot, lasting fire." A Works Progress Administration source shows that one pit master there preferred "hickory or other hardwood[s]" such as oak and pecan.[233] Hardwoods burn longer and hotter and provide more flavor to foods through the smoke that is produced than softwoods. Historically, hickory is the most commonly used hardwood for barbecuing in the South, followed by oak. Pecan, which produces a milder smoke taste than hickory, is also used.[234]

Hurston's Eatonville barbecue scene in *Their Eyes Were Watching God* features two pit masters, Hambo and Pearson, who supervised the preparation of the barbecue pit and the burning down of "oak" wood into "a glowing bed of coals."[235] In the 1930s, pit master Crummit started burning hardwood as early as 5:00 a.m. and "thereafter [fed it] watchfully, just enough to keep the coals red and a little flame spurting." At 6:00 a.m., he had his crew put "hogs skinned, cleaned, and split into halves along the backbone, upon the iron rods that cross the pit."[236] A 1940 article says, "The intense infrared rays" that the red-hot charcoal produces give barbecued meat its incredible "mouth-watering" taste. Southern pit masters say the hardwood charcoal heat "penetrate[s] the meat and develop[s] its best flavors."[237] Native Americans described *barbacoa* as a bed one put the dead on to reach utopia. In short, southern barbecuing meant placing meat on a rack or a revolving spit above live coals to obtain a heavenly experience.[238]

COOKING AND BASTING

The key to good barbecue is a constant basting of the meat while it slow cooks. No southern barbecue could be considered done unless the meat was "saturated with blistering sauces." Cooks repeatedly baste the barbecuing meat until it is an "aromatic brown."[239] In *Their Eyes Were Watching God*, Hurston describes a group of men gathering around a barbecue pit and basting three hogs all night long. She writes, "Hambo and Pearson had full charge while the others helped out with the turning the meat now and then while Hambo swabbed it all over with the sauce. In between times they told stories, laughed and told more stores and sung songs. They cut all sorts of capers and whiffed the meat as it slowly came to perfection with the seasoning penetrating to the bone."[240]

Basting sauces differ across the South. A basting recipe that former slave Louis Hughes recalls from the 1830s contains "butter, pepper, salt, and vinegar."[241] The butter prevents the baste from rolling completely off the barbecuing meat when it is mopped on. The pit masters who ran

Harvey E. Slade at a Presbyterian church barbecue, Tallahassee, Florida, circa 1940. *Courtesy of State Archives of Florida, Florida Memory.*

A barbecue on Farmers' Day at the equipment division at Gibbs Corporation, Tallahassee, Florida, 1948. *Courtesy of State Archives of Florida, Florida Memory.*

the barbecue operation for his master "basted the carcasses with" the sauce "until the meat were ready to serve," says Hughes.[242]

Martha McCulloch-Williams, author of *Dishes and Beverages of the Old South*, published in 1913, calls for twelve hours of cooking time over hot coals from "midnight to noon next day, usually."[243] In the book, she shares her father's sauce that he gleaned from an old plantation pit master. "Two pounds sweet lard, melted in a brass kettle, with one pound beaten, not ground, black pepper, a pint of small fiery red peppers, nubbed and stewed soft in water barely cover, a spoonful of herbs in powder—he would never tell what they were—and a quart and a pint of the strongest apple vinegar, with a little salt."[244] Combine the ingredients and simmer them for half an hour while the meat is cooking. Then lightly apply the basting sauce to each side of the meat with a fresh, clean mop, preventing any from dropping on the coals and thereby causing smoke and ash to form on the barbecued meat.[245]

Mop Sauce Basting Recipe
(for use on 10 pounds of ribs)

1 bottle of ketchup (8 ounces)
2 cups vinegar
2 tablespoons Worcestershire sauce
1 cup French mustard
1 tablespoon salt
1 tablespoon pepper

Mix ingredients and baste with mop every 15 minutes. Meat cooked over hot coal fire should be done in 45 minutes. When meat is done use old fashioned sauce.[246]

SAUCE

Crummit's basting sauce contained "vinegar, brown sugar, cayenne pepper, [and] a little garlic." A WPA record goes on to say that he made a "swab by tying a clean rag around the end of a clean stick. With it he smears the sauce over the top side of the halfhog. After the meat has cooked a little, Dad forks it over, so that the sauced side is towards the coals, and he swabs more sauce on the other side. After six hours of saucing, turning, and cooking, the hog is ready to be cut and served."[247] A WPA source says the process takes "fifteen to twenty hours," with "nearly half that time" preparing to cook.[248] Erwin Duke Stephens describes seeing black pit masters who "swabbed" barbecuing hogs on both sides "with a mixture of apple cider vinegar, and ground red pepper." He says the basting process in his part of the South "gives the cooked meat a sour flavor so prized by eastern Carolina folks. The smoke from the dripping fat on the coals also enhances the flavor."[249]

A 1928 article on the southern barbecue also suggested a basting concoction that included "a good deal of pepper, mustard, pickles, and vinegar" in a sauce that is "thin and generally much too hot stuff."[250] Another basting sauce contained "usually fifteen or more ingredients," according to a WPA writer.[251] A 1938 article printed the basting recipe of two rural black pit masters. Their basting or "moppin" recipe contained "two gallons of vinegar, two pounds of butter, with salt and pepper to taste."[252]

The Williams family opened the Golden Rule restaurant in 1891. During the Great Depression, it remained a popular family-operated barbecue and beer joint on what was known as the Atlanta Highway. The Golden Rule thrived with the development of a tomato-based sauce that is popular in the Birmingham region of the South. The Golden Rule is still open today.[253]

Parts of southern Georgia also tended toward a tomato-based sauce, but in northern Georgia, the western Carolinas and the Lowcountry (from Columbia to Charleston), the region's German influence led to a preference for a mustard-based sauce as, historically, Germans have preferred pork with mustard. Those living in the eastern Carolinas favored vinegar-based pepper sauces.[254]

Barbecue Pork Sauce Recipe

2 cans of tomato paste
1 tablespoon Worcestershire sauce
Juice of one lemon
1 cup vinegar
½ cup French mustard
1 tablespoon salt
1 teaspoon black pepper
1 tablespoon crushed pepper
2 sprigs of garlic

Mix ingredients well. Add to a pint of beef broth and a pint of water. Cook 35 minutes. Add 2 tablespoons of mixed spice, strain and serve over hot meat. [255]

Old Fashioned Barbeque Sauce Recipe[256]

2 small cans of tomato paste
1 tablespoon of Worcestershire sauce
Juice of 1 lemon
1 cup vinegar
½ cup French mustard
1 tablespoon salt

1 teaspoon of black pepper
1 tablespoon of crushed pepper
2 tablespoons mixed spice
2 sprigs of garlic
1 pint of beef broth
1 pint of water

Take tomato paste, Worcestershire sauce, lemon juice, vinegar, French mustard, salt, black pepper, crushed pepper, and garlic. Mix well and add to a beef broth and water. Cook thirty-five minutes, and add mixed spice, strain and serve hot over meat.[257]

CULTURE

A sugar plantation in Clewiston, Florida, used the promise of regular barbecues to recruit black laborers from Arkansas. A circular with pictures of "barbecues and weekly entertainments for" workers "promised good steady jobs for 300 Negro men, free transportation to Florida, and $3 a day compensation with meals and lodging furnished."[258]

A nefarious relationship existed among electoral politics, barbecues and black laborers in Hurston's Jim Crow South. Records from the period show that southern "planters and owners of turpentine [camps]" forced black workers "to the polls and voted them in gangs" on election day. In some voting districts, employers held all-night election eve feasts where barbecue, beer "and whisky by the barrel" were served. Then on election day, they "carefully guarded" and marched those who attended the barbecue "to the polls by the beat of the drums" to ensure all voted for the desired candidate.[259]

In her own work, Hurston often pairs barbecued meats with liquor and/ or moonshine, as well as sweets. In *Seraph on the Suwanee*, set near citrus plantations in west Florida, a group of black laborers clears five acres of land for their black foreman, Jim, who supplies them with ingredients for a barbecue and shotgun shells to kill hogs. Hurston explains in the novel that stealing hogs for a barbecue had been easy because so "many Crackers" let them "run wild in the woods until just before" hog-killing time as a way of saving on pig feed. "If a big barbeque was going to be held on his place," Jim did not want to know "nothing about where all that meat came from."[260] He

Above: F.M. Gay's annual plantation barbecue, circa 1930. *Courtesy of Library of Congress*.

Right: A staff person eating at the inaugural barbecue for Florida governor Warren, 1949. *Courtesy of State Archives of Florida, Florida Memory*.

The Burgert brothers' moonshine still in their house attic, Tampa, Florida, 1920. *Courtesy of State Archives of Florida, Florida Memory.*

Jugs of moonshine and distillery equipment, Jacksonville, circa 1935. *Courtesy of State Archives of Florida, Florida Memory.*

paid the work crew only "ten gallons of moonshine at a dollar and a half a gallon, ten pounds of sugar, two ten-cent bags of salt, a quart of vinegar, and some red pepper" to build a house in rural west Florida.[261] Similarly, in 1925, law enforcement officers near Atlanta seized "500 bottles" of "home brew" from a post of the American Legion barbecue. Police "had received several complaints about the sale of the liquor at the barbeque."[262]

Hurston describes barbecues, particularly those with plenty of moonshine or homebrew on hand, as "boisterous event[s]." She uses the expression "kicking up racket like niggers at a barbecue" to describe a rowdy group.[263] The officers who carried out the raid on the barbecue near Atlanta said the homebrew "was located some distance from the scene of the barbecue and that there was no one around the cache at the time of the seizure except some negroes who made an immediate departure." The police found large batches of beer "in gallon containers and bottles."[264]

In the novel *The Color Purple*, author Alice Walker provides a rich description of the pairing of liquor and barbecue in a southern juke joint in the 1930s and 1940s.[265] Harpo and Swain stocked their new juke joint with liquor and barbecue. Harpo purchased "cold drinks, he got barbecue, he got chitlins, [and he] got store-bought bread."[266] The business took off

Preparation for a barbecue in celebration of the new courthouse, Bartow, Florida, 1909. *Courtesy of State Archives of Florida, Florida Memory.*

Wainwright celebration barbecue, Starke, Florida, 1946. *Courtesy of State Archives of Florida, Florida Memory.*

after Harpo got Shug Avery, a renowned singer, to agree to perform. That first Saturday night, "so many folks come they couldn't git in."[267] Harpo would go on to gain a bunch of weight while working at the juke joint "drinking homebrew and eating leftover barbecue."[268]

Hurston enjoyed a barbecue while doing fieldwork. Near Titusville in Brevard County, Florida, giving someone "a big hunk of barbecue" when they wanted a sandwich was a way to curry favor.[269] Similarly, honored guests in the folklore she collected move without restriction at a barbecue and have access to the host who distributes the best cuts of meat. In contrast, the marginalized have restricted movement and limited access to the host and get the worst cuts of the barbecued meat.[270]

It became customary in southern sawmill towns and turpentine camps for a juke that sold barbecue to serve as a place of entertainment for men to unwind. Black entrepreneurs owned these jukes (sometimes spelled jooks) in the segregated South and provided a place where laborers could eat their daily meals. "The grilled chicken, spare ribs, spicy pork, and whole range of smoky barbecued meat cooked so well in these places…are a continuum of the cooking that males did, beginning with those on plantations," writes anthropologist Anne Yentsch.[271]

Hurston describes barbecue as a community event instead of an individual or family event. The folk tales that she collected about a crow,

A 1940 juke joint. *Courtesy of Library of Congress.*

Living quarters and the juke joint for migratory workers, Belle Glade, Florida, 1941. *Courtesy of Library of Congress.*

a character in the story about a community of common animals, is a case in point. Crow says, "Well, brothers and sisters, since we'se all here at one time, you know Sister Speckled Hen is having a grand barbecue and fish fry down on Front Street and Beale—why not let's have one grand consolidated, amalgamated fraternal parade down to her place and enjoy the consequences?"[272]

Similarly, Hurston talks about a barbecue following a "log-rolling," preparing and placing logs to build a new home. Her description of a log-rolling sounds similar to a hog killing except the work concludes with barbecued meat and perhaps moonshine as barter for collective labor. After the labor is completed, the recipient of the help hosts a barbecue to thank neighbors for participating in the group effort.[273]

SWEETS AND MEATS

As mentioned earlier, in *Their Eyes Were Watching God*, Hurston pairs barbecued meats with sweet and savory tastes, with the men in charge of barbecuing a whole hog and the women baking pies, cakes and sweet potato pudding or pone.

Cutting pies and cakes at a barbecue, 1940. *Courtesy of Library of Congress.*

Black Chocolate Cake Recipe
Serves 15

½ cup shortening
½ cup brown sugar
¾ cup sour milk
2 eggs
2 squares chocolate, melted
2 cups flour
¾ teaspoon baking soda
¼ teaspoon salt
1 teaspoon vanilla

Dissolve baking soda in 1 teaspoon of water then mix with the ingredients in the order listed above beating eggs well. Bake at 375°F for 45 to 50 minutes in a cake pan. Let cool before frosting and serving. Use the chocolate frosting of your choice.[274]

Peach Cobbler Recipe
Serves 6 to 8

1 quart peaches
1½ cups sugar
1 cup water
3 tablespoons butter
1 egg
1 cup flour
¼ teaspoon salt
2 teaspoons baking powder
½ cup milk

Peel peaches, remove stones, and cut the fruit into small pieces. Add 1¼ cups of sugar and the water. Bake closely covered in a shallow dish until the fruit is tender. Cream the butter and rest of sugar. Gradually add the well beaten egg. Mix and sift the dry ingredients and combine alternately with the milk to the creamed mixture, blending thoroughly. Pour over the hot fruit and bake 20–25 minutes in a moderately hot oven.[275]

"MOTHER THOMPSON'S BLOCK" AND ENTREPRENEURS

From approximately the turn of the century to the 1940s, Mother Thompson operated a barbecue stand in Coconut Grove, a Miami, Florida neighborhood. Born a slave in Griffin, Georgia, in 1855, Thompson recalls that when "freedom come, white folks call all the colored people and told them their ages and turned them loose. It was a long time for we come into the knowledge of how to make a living." She goes on to say, "When I come to Florida I worked at anything that come t' hand…When I married Brother Thompson we bought a farm outa Rockdale. I drove the beans and tomatoes to the wharf [on my bicycle] and put them on the boat, or" drove them on the bike to the depot or wherever her husband was selling them. "Whenever I got hold of a dollar, I saved it," and in those days, if you made "$15 you was doing big business." She earned on average $8 to $10 a week and decided "to invest what I had in real estate" and purchase a house and some buildings where I sold barbecue and operated other businesses. "My husband kept wonderin' what I was doing with my money til I took him to see" what she had bought and showed "him I had the key." Thompson explains her success: "I live by the word and I can say I never sold no one nor give no one no liquor to help with his downfall [and profit] my businesses. I ain't never had to do that and God has truly prospered me." In 1949, Thompson owned what people in Coconut Grove called "Mother Thompson's Block," which was a row of businesses including a barbecue stand, grocery store, chicken and fish market, beauty shop, tailor shop, general store, barbershop and poolroom.[276]

CONCLUSION

The legacy of barbecue in Florida is that it developed from American, African and European ingredients, cooking techniques and styles of eating. Today, no single ethnic group can claim that its members were the original barbecue pit masters because the art of barbecuing developed over hundreds of years from the complex amalgamation of the culinary contributions of various ethnic groups. Barbecuing is like the history of other cooking techniques. It was a creolized culinary art form in which various traditions merged and the various new traditions resemble aspects of the original traditions. The transformation of the ingredients used in jerk seasonings, dry rubs, basting sauces and barbecue sauces is a good example of the type of changes described above. Next to the woods used in a barbecue pit, seasoning and marinating have the most important influence on the taste of what is cooked. The taste of and access to the ingredients used in barbecuing food changes slowly over time, place and space.

During the antebellum period, enslaved Africans held the mantle of the most skilled pit masters, barbecuing hogs for those in the big house as well as the slave quarters. The use of black pit masters among white southerners decreased after the abolition of slavery and during the period of Jim Crow segregation. The Great Migration and the arrivals to the Americas of immigrants with different barbecuing traditions starting around World War I and World War II have had the effect of slowly disseminating different barbecue techniques inside and outside the African American cooking traditions. The same is true with the introduction of new barbecue methods after 1965, when the U.S. government changed immigration policies that increased the number of non-European immigrants coming to Florida from the Caribbean. Hurston's work shows that by the Great Depression, the definition of an expert pit master no longer meant an African American, as it had during the antebellum period.

Today, barbecuing has become more egalitarian and has morphed into a quintessentially American tradition used to commemorate some of our most patriotic holidays like Memorial Day and the Fourth of July. Unlike the food traditions surrounding Thanksgiving and Christmas, barbecuing since the colonial period in the Americas has been a labor-intensive special-occasion event cooked and celebrated outdoors. This is because during the hot seasons of the year, preparing food in a hot kitchen for hours for large numbers of people would have been difficult for most cooks to endure. Barbecuing on the Fourth of July and Memorial Day must have been a natural adaptation after the end of the colonial period. Finally, corn on the cob, corn bread, coleslaw, greens, potato dishes, beer, alcohol, iced tea, coffee, ice cream and pies are among the most enduring dishes, drinks and sweets made/and or bought and served at barbecues today.

Florida Slaw Recipe
Serves 3

1 grapefruit, peeled and sectioned
2 cups shredded cabbage
½ cup Mother's mayonnaise
1 teaspoon salt
½ teaspoon celery seed

Have grapefruit and cabbage well chilled. Combine all ingredients lightly. For variety, substitute 1 cup orange or tangerine sections for the grapefruit.[277]

AFTERWORD

This book has focused on Hurston's research and writing on Florida foodways. However, Hurston did a great deal of research in which she compared and contrasted her own culinary roots with those of the people of the Caribbean, as well as other parts of the U.S. South. I thought it would be relevant to include this content as an afterword, considering that the state of Florida has had a large influx of people from the Caribbean and other regions of the South from time and memorial. The afterword looks at food and spirituality topics that Hurston, as a preacher's kid, had a continuous interest in.

FIELDWORK IN THE CARIBBEAN

During her professional career as an anthropologist, Hurston conducted fieldwork in Jamaica and Haiti. In 1936, she received a prestigious Guggenheim Fellowship to study religion in the Caribbean. While living there for two years, she wrote *Their Eyes Were Watching God* over a seven-week period. From 1947 to 1948, she lived on the Caribbean coast of Honduras in Puerto Cortes. She went there to research the black experience in Central America. While there, she wrote a great deal of *Seraph on the Suwanee*, which has nothing to do with Honduras.

From her time doing fieldwork in the Caribbean, she developed writings in a number of genres that provide a rich body of work on food and African cultural survivals in that region.

The religious traditions of the West African kingdoms of Ile, Ife, Oyo and Hausa can be seen throughout the Americas. The Yoruba, who today are one of the largest ethnic groups in West Africa, consist of more than thirty million individuals. They have made the most significant influence on African religions practiced in the Caribbean, Louisiana, Florida and other parts of the U.S. South.[278] Before Africans arrived in colonial America, they had a well-developed religious life that included symbolic foods served in ritualistic ways. West and Central African religions honored and acknowledged God and the community's relationship to the spiritual world in everyday activities and on religious holidays and feasts. Africans held a belief that an honorable person showed reverence to God, community leaders, friends and family through the use of food. As a result, West African ancestors incorporated food into their religious rituals and celebrations.

Examples from different parts of West Africa and during different centuries illustrate this. Just before the planting of yams, villagers along the Niger River contributed an abundance of palm wine and game to a yearly yam planting festival. The inhabitants of the city of Accra, in the Kingdom of Ghana, commonly hunted and prepared wild hare. The Igbo, Hausa and Mande offered fowl to gods at religious holidays and ceremonies. In mid-nineteenth-century West Africa, the Brass People observed food-centered funeral practices that contained similarities to traditions later observed in Haiti. At burial time, a Brass priest threw "herbs over the body" of the deceased, and a "bottle of rum, together with some cooked eatables, are generally placed on the grave over the head" of the deceased.[279]

RELIGIOUS RITUALS IN THE CARIBBEAN

Hurston's fieldwork also points to a focus on the chicken wing in religious ceremonies in Haiti, in which the high priest "broke the wings of one of the chickens," says Hurston.[280] Vodou in Haiti originated in the eighteenth century in the French slave colony of Saint-Domingue, where the French suppressed the practice of African religions and forced enslaved Africans to convert to the Catholic religion. Vodou incorporated elements of Catholic, Native American and African religious beliefs, as well as Freemasonry.[281]

In the practice of vodou, observers worship the supreme being, Bondye, along with the worship of several smaller beings. Haitians perform dance and food rituals as an aid to worship and to communicate with the spirit world.[282] Most of the vodou ceremonies of the 1940s lasted for several hours, starting at midnight and lasting until daybreak. Food was served at the ceremonies as offerings as well as a way to enable the participants to continue through several hours of dancing, singing and other aspects of the sometimes physically demanding religious rituals. Coffee, alcohol, nuts (like pistachio nuts and peanuts), coconut, grain (such as rice and millet) and chicken are among the most commonly mentioned foods and drinks observed at vodou ceremonies.[283] One wonders about the significance of, for example, the chicken wings in African folklore and the belief that the African's soul flies back to Africa after one dies in the Americas. Enslaved Africans particularly held this belief throughout the diaspora. Filmmaker Julie Dash touches on it in the documentary *Daughters of the Dust*, the first full-length film released by an African American woman.[284]

During fieldwork in the Caribbean, Hurston found the common belief that "once Africans could all fly…Many of them were brought to Jamaica to be slaves, but they never were slaves. They flew back to Africa." She adds, "Those who ate salt had to stay in Jamaica and be slaves, because they were too heavy to fly." Masters forced enslaved Africans to consume salted fish (cod, mackerel and herring) and pork as food rations. Thus, Africans viewed the consumption of these foreign foods as one's acceptance of their oppressor's way of life. Those who accepted oppression proved unworthy and lost the right to return to Africa.[285]

While doing fieldwork in Port-au-Prince, Haiti, Hurston attended a ceremony in which followers of vodou cooked white pigeons and a pair of white chickens for all the gods and goddesses to eat.[286] A similar meal was given to the god Legba Attibon, to whom followers gave a roasted chicken.[287] Similarly, the Feast of the Dead (also called the Festival of the Dead and the Day of the Dead) in Haiti included white pigeons and chickens. Hurston explains that followers cooked the chickens and pigeons in olive oil without seasoning, especially salt. She writes, "This reminded me of my experiences in Jamaica and how it was felt that salt was offensive to the dead," so the priest put the birds cooked in olive oil and without salt on a white plate and "offered them to the dead with tremendous earnestness and dignity."[288] "After that the plates were paraded around the two chairs and buried with the food on them."[289] On the menu of the Haitian ceremony the Tête de L'eau (Head of the Water), one finds roast turkey and chicken.[290] The priest in charge of a ceremony selected the chicken parts necessary for the ceremony, which were "the feet, head and wings of the sacrificed chickens. Should any of these parts be missing, Legba would be very angry and would consider the ceremony as of no worth," writes anthropologist George E. Simpson, a contemporary of Hurston.[291] Hurston's scholarly peers Odette M. Rigaud, Alfred Métraux and Rhoda Métraux also conducted fieldwork in Haiti around the 1940s. They write, "Legba's food is barbecued," and his "food consists of a rooster and a hen cut into small pieces, grilled with sweet potatoes, yams, malanga (a type of yam), giraumon (pumpkins)" and other foods.[292]

YAMS AND SWEET POTATOES

Hurston provides a detailed description of the annual feast of the yam celebration in Haiti observed in October. She recalls, "We had to buy the yams for the feast on the last day in October" and used "olive oil to cook the yams" and the other foods prepared for the celebration.[293] People of good conduct had the trusted responsibility of preparing food for the spirits. The cook began the work early in the morning the day before the feast, supervising assistants who helped cook large pots of the food offered at the ceremony and eaten by the participants. One could see cooks preparing large pots of rice and beans and barbecued corn, sweet potatoes, bananas, yams, pumpkins and other foods.[294]

The yams were cooked in olive oil and then offered to the gods before anyone could eat them. Participants were seated on a couch made of banana leaves, where they waited until the food was ready to be served to them.[295] The scene Hurston describes is similar to the New Yam Festival described in Chinua Achebe's award-winning novel *Things Fall Apart* set in a small Ibo village in turn-of-the-century Nigeria. Based on fieldwork done in Haiti in the late 1930s, Hurston writes that the Rada cult, the Congo, the Petro, the Ibo and Congo Petro all over Haiti had to honor the yam once each year.[296] She goes on to say:

> *When the word came that the yams were ready, the houngan* [leading male priest] *sprinkled flour all around the couch* [made of banana leaves]. *Then he went into the hounfort* [temple] *and the food was carried in to him and he offered some of it to the loa* [spirits]. *Then everyone was served and we passed the rest of the night singing and amusing ourselves.*[297]

Another vodou ceremony Hurston observed in Haiti included roasted sweet potatoes. She notes how the food at this ceremony for the Spirit Papa Legaba had to be prepared. "All of his food must be roasted," and the yams and other foods had to be "put in the Macoute [a big bag made from palms] and tied to the limb of a tree that has been baptized in the name of Papa Legba."[298]

Haitian Sweet Potato Pudding Recipe
Makes 10 servings

2½ cups mashed hot sweet potatoes
2 eggs
3 tablespoons shortening
½ cup milk
1 tablespoon flour
2 cups sugar
2 teaspoons double-acting baking powder
¼ teaspoon salt
¼ teaspoon nutmeg
3 tablespoons chopped peanuts
1 cup brown sugar
½ cup butter or margarine

Mix sweet potato with well-beaten eggs. Add shortening, add milk, mixing thoroughly after each addition. Sift together flour, sugar, baking powder, salt and nutmeg. Add to first mixture, beat it in well, and then add the nuts. Pour into mold lined with a mixture of brown sugar and butter or margarine. Bake in moderate oven (350°F.) about one hour.[299]

FISH

Cooked fish was a common dish served during African American religious events in New Orleans, Hurston writes. During the rainy season from late February to early March, people in New Orleans's Lower Ninth Ward feared a flood. A religious leader in that section of the Crescent City named Mother

Seal "exhorted all of her followers to pin their faith in her. All they need do is believe in her and come to her and eat the blessed fish she cooked for them [Hurston does not state how Seal prepared the fish] and there would be no flood." Mother Seal's message to her congregants, Hurston records, was that God "put oars in the fishes hands. Eat this fish and you needn't fear the flood no more than a fish would."[300]

CORN

In Haiti, Hurston attended vodou ceremonies and learned the accompanying songs and food offerings, one of which was corn.[301] In one place she attended "ceremonies nearly every day...sometimes two or three in the same day." She writes that the elaborate rituals "astonished" her, and she took note that one vodou ritual for the dead called for roasted coarse cornmeal. The priest took roasted cornmeal and offered it at a ceremonial fire while chanting.[302] At Arcahaie, Haiti, Hurston observed ceremonies in which priests offered roasted corn and cornmeal on the altar of a deity.[303] Of the deity Guedé, Hurston writes that he eats "parched corn like his devotees."[304] Similarly, Rigaud, Métraux and Métraux found during their fieldwork in Haiti in the 1940s that a "special dish" for Guedé "consisted of roasted maize grains and peanuts, avocados, and cassava."[305] Simpson, too, describes observing a ritual meal in which the high priests offered roasted corn and a cornmeal dish at a ceremony.[306]

At Arcahaie, Hurston observed ceremonies in which priests offered roasted peanuts to deities. Legba Attibon "is the first god in all Haiti in point of service," writes Hurston. "Every service...for whatever purpose must be preceded by a service to Legba. They say he has a brother, however, who eats his food from a...bowl made from half a calabash (a type of gourd). All of his food must be roasted."[307] She observed priests serving the deity roasted peanuts, bananas and sweet potatoes. She adds, "The deity Guedé eats roasted peanuts and parched corn like his devotees."[308] Rigaud, Métraux and Métraux made similar findings, calling roasted peanuts one of Guedé's favorite dishes. In contrast to Hurston and other scholars mentioned here, Simpson is alone in observing the use of pistachio nuts in Haitian vodou ceremonies done around the same time.[309]

At vodou ceremonies, Haitians offered beans and rice to deities. At Aux Cayes (known today as Les Cayes), Hurston noted women preparing "great heaps" of peas, string beans, rice and other foods for a religious ceremony.[310] She found that in Haiti, some buried the dead with "parched peas" placed in the coffin as a "precaution for keeping [the ghost]" of the deceased in his or her grave.[311] Similarly, she observed cooked white rice given as an offering at ceremonies.[312]

While doing fieldwork in Louisiana, Hurston recorded a story about "a pleasure dance" held in New Orleans, "the hoodoo [or vodou] capital of America."[313] Some suspected that it was "a hoodoo dance" because it occurred in "Congo Square and included the beating of drums with the shin bone of a donkey and everybody dance[d] like they do in Hayti." The event was held the first Friday night of each month, and participants dined on "crab gumbo and rice." Hurston writes, "The white people come look on, and think they see all, when they only see a dance."[314]

CONCLUSION

Hurston's and other scholars' fieldwork and writings show that food has been central in African diaspora religious traditions. For centuries, it has been part of the transaction between the believer and the divine in the request for supernatural intervention in the natural world. Author Yvonne Daniel puts it this way: "Food is the last element of most services; it is a reciprocal 'present' that worshipers first give to" an all-powerful creator.[315] It creates bonds among people and between people and the spiritual world. Different religions have over time defined what sacred food is and what the preferred food is of the supernatural being they want to communicate with and worship.[316] Differences exist in terms of religions, regions and preferences for color, shape and the ingredients added to a dish to make it sweet or savory, bland or spicy, animal or plant-based. In some African religious traditions, foods that resembled a god in shape, color and texture pleased them and became sacred foods. These were also foods considered to have the ability to refresh and energize the gods that practitioners would wear out with request. In Haitian vodou, the spirits are particular about the food they are offered during ceremonies.[317] Indeed, food played an important part in the vodou ceremonies that Hurston and other scholars observed. Coffee, rum, liquor, plantains, bananas, sweet potatoes, yams, roasted corn and cornmeal, cassava cakes, pistachio nuts, chopped coconut, grain (such as rice and millet) and chicken are among the most commonly mentioned foods and drinks observed at vodou ceremonies.[318]

Through oral histories, the elders teach the next generation how to prepare these foods in ways pleasing to god and man. People who are pure are trusted with the responsibility of preparing or supervising the preparation of religious food in abundance for a special occasion such as the burial of the dead or a religious holiday.[319] In the African and African diaspora tradition, sacred food is well-seasoned plant and animal food and the best of one's roasted or barbecued animals, particularly some kind of poultry parts like wings. In the Caribbean, roasted corn and rum made from sugar cane and other liquors are marked features of vodou ceremonies. In contrast, sweet desserts made with sugar cane and pork-laden dishes are a hallmark of the food blacks make for church events and religious holidays in the southern United States. The preparation of poultry dishes and yam or sweet potato dishes are religious culinary traditions that the two regions have in common from their shared West and Central African heritage.

NOTES

CHAPTER 1

1. Zora Neale Hurston, *Folklore, Memoirs, and Other Writings* [online] (New York: Library of America, 1995), 577–78.
2. Ibid., 578.
3. Ibid.
4. Ibid.
5. Frederick Douglass Opie, *Hog and Hominy: Soul Food from Africa to America* (New York: Columbia University Press, 2008), 23, 47.
6. Hurston, *Folklore*, 577.
7. Dr. David Driskell was raised in the 1930s in Rutherford County, North Carolina. Like Hurston, he would go on to attend Howard University and have a career as an artist, professor and writer. In speaking about his childhood and race relations in rural North Carolina, Driskell says blacks and whites lived "side-by-side" and depended on one another for their survival, which is "something you don't hear written about or talked about." Frederick Douglass Opie interview with David Driskell, September 2011.
8. Carla Kaplan, ed. and collector, *Zora Neale Hurston: A Life in Letters*, 1st ed. (New York: Doubleday, 2002), 773.
9. Hurston, *Folklore*, 567.
10. Kaplan, *Zora Neale Hurston*, 773; Hurston, *Folklore*, 569.

11. Pamela Bordelon, ed. and with a biographical essay, *Go Gator and Muddy the Water: Writings by Zora Neale Hurston from the Federal Writers' Project* (New York: W.W. Norton, 1999), 3–4.

12. Ibid., 5.

13. Hurston, *Folklore*, 575–76.

14. Ibid., 575; John Edgerton, *Southern Food: At Home, on the Road, in History*, with a special assist from Ann Bleidt Edgerton and with photographs by Al Clayton (New York: Alfred A. Knopf, 1987), 37.

15. Hurston, *Folklore*, 571.

16. Ibid., 847.

17. Ibid., 579.

18. Ibid., 813.

19. Ibid., 754.

20. Marjorie Kinnan Rawlings, *Cross Creek Cookery* (New York: Fireside, 1942), 57.

21. Hurston, *Folklore*, 571.

22. Ibid.

23. Ibid.

24. *Florida Agriculturist* 19 (June 1892), 362. Google eBook.

25. *Pittsburgh Courier*, June 10, 1911.

26. Ibid.

27. Ibid.

28. *Baltimore Afro-American*, June 21, 1918.

29. Ibid.

30. Hurston, *Folklore*, 827.

31. Ibid., 816.

32. Ibid., 574.

33. *Atlanta Constitution*, February 5, 1924.

34. Hurston, *Folklore*, 821.

35. Ibid., 820.

36. Ibid., 580.

37. Ibid.

38. *Florida Agriculturist* 19 (June 1892).

39. Opie, *Hog and Hominy*, 4, 5, 25.

40. Mandy Gibson, Kentucky, Works Project Administration Federal Writers' Project, *Slave Narratives* [database online] (Provo, UT: Ancestry. com, 2000). Original data from Works Project Administration Federal Writers' Project, *Slave Narratives: A Folk History of Slavery in the United States from Interviews with Former Slaves* (Washington, D.C.: n.d.) [hereafter WPA].

41. Harvey A. Levenstein, *Revolution at the Table: The Transformation of the American Diet* (New York: Oxford University Press, 1988), 27.

42. Margaret Cussler and Mary L. de Give, *'Twixt the Cup and the Lip: Psychological and Socio-Cultural Factors Affecting Food Habits* (Washington, D.C.: Consortium Press, 1972, first edition, 1952), 77; Evan Kleiman interview with Marc Levinson, Good Food on KCRW Los Angeles Public Radio, February 2013.

43. Marc Levinson, *The Great A&P and the Struggle for Small Business in America* (New York: Hill and Wang, 2011), 49–50; Kleiman interview with Levinson.

44. Hurston, *Folklore*, 571.

45. Zora Neale Hurston, *Their Eyes Were Watching God: A Novel* (New York: HarperCollins, 2010).

46. Hurston, *Folklore*, 599.

47. Dennis Brindell Fradin and Judith Bloom Fradin, *Zora! The Life of Zora Neale Hurston* (New York: Clarion Books, 2012), 11–14.

48. Ibid.

49. Hurston, *Folklore*, 587.

50. *Daily Boston Globe,* July 12, 1928.

51. On the fight between Zora and her stepmother that led to her father's decision to send her away to boarding school in Jacksonville, see Bordelon, *Go Gator*, 4–7; Fradin and Fradin, *Zora!*, 19–21; Kaplan, *Zora Neale Hurston*, 39–40.

52. Hurston, *Folklore*, 628.

53. Ibid., 621.

54. Ibid., 628.

55. Ibid., 630.

56. Ibid., 631.

57. Kaplan, *Zora Neale Hurston*, 50.

58. *New York Amsterdam News,* September 27, 1947.

CHAPTER 2

59. Hurston, *Their Eyes Were Watching God*, 83.

60. Opie, *Hog and Hominy*, 78–79.

61. Ibid., 109.

62. Ibid., 90.

63. Mark Kurlansky, ed., *The Food of a Younger Land: A Portrait of American Food—Before the National Highway System, Before Chain Restaurants, and Before*

Frozen Food, When the Nation's Food Was Seasonal, Regional, and Traditional—From the Lost WPA Files (New York: Penguin, 2009), 147–55.

64. *Pittsburgh Courier,* June 29, 1929.

65. *Chicago Defender*, November 30, 1929.

66. Zora Neale Hurston, *Seraph on the Suwanee* (New York: Scribner's, 1948), 64.

67. Rawlings, *Cross Creek Cookery*, 127–28.

68. Hurston, *Folklore*, 64.

69. Ibid., 136.

70. Ibid., 132.

71. Ibid., 133.

72. Ibid., 132–33.

73. Ibid., 96–97.

74. Rawlings, *Cross Creek Cookery*, 28–29.

75. Hurston, *Folklore*, 720.

76. Opie, *Hog and Hominy*, 4–5, 20–22.

77. Hurston, *Seraph on the Suwanee*, 216.

78. Ibid., 263–64.

79. Ibid., 216, 72.

80. Hurston, *Folklore*, 69.

81. Rawlings, *Cross Creek Cookery*, 23.

82. Ibid., 55.

83. Judith A. Carney and Richard Nicholas Rosomoff, *In the Shadow of Slavery: Africa's Botanical Legacy in the Atlantic World* (Berkeley: University of California Press, 2010), 141–44.

84. Hurston, *Folklore*, 720.

85. Ibid., 22.

86. Ibid., 695.

87. Ibid., 63–64.

88. Opie, *Hog and Hominy*, 37, 78–79.

89. Ibid., 28–29.

90. Hurston, *Their Eyes Were Watching God*, 7.

91. Recipe adapted from *The Savannah Cook Book: A Collection of Old-Fashioned Recipes from Colonial Kitchens* (New York: Farrar & Rinehart Incorporated, 1933), collected and edited by Harriet Ross Colquitt, with an introduction by Ogden Nash and decorations by Florence Olmstead. Cover illustration designed by Mildred Howells, daughter of William Dean Howells. Originally published in 1933. Reprint of the eighth edition, 1974.

92. Hurston, *Folklore*, 69.

93. Ibid., 251.

94. Ibid., 42–43.

95. Ibid., 255.

96. Ibid., 262.

97. Hurston, *Their Eyes Were Watching God*, 183.

98. Opie, *Hog and Hominy*, 11.

99. Pearl Bowser and Joan Eckstein, *A Pinch of Soul in Book Form* (New York: Avon Books, 1969), 13.

100. *Chicago Daily Tribune*, April 6, 1923.

101. Hurston, *Their Eyes Were Watching God*, 94.

102. Hurston, *Folklore*, 881.

103. Ibid., 293.

104. Ibid., 751–52.

105. Opie, *Hog and Hominy*, 77–79.

106. Recipe adapted from Rawlings, *Cross Creek Cookery*, 124; and Joyce LaFray, *Country Cookin': Famous Recipes from Famous Places* (n.p.: Seaside Publishing, 1990), 76.

107. Opie, *Hog and Hominy*, 7.

108. Frederick Law Olmsted, *The Cotton Kingdom: A Traveler's Observations on Cotton and Slavery in the American Slave States: Based Upon Three Former Volumes of Journeys and Investigations by the Same Author*, edited by Arthur M. Schlesinger Sr., introduction by Lawrence N. Powell (New York: Modern Library, Random House, Inc., 1984), 71.

109. Hurston, *Their Eyes Were Watching God*, 62.

110. Hurston, *Folklore*, 882–83.

111. Ibid., 894.

112. Hurston, *Seraph on the Suwanee*, 227–28.

113. Ibid., 74.

114. *Atlanta Daily World*, September 16, 1949.

115. *Baltimore Afro-American*, January 20, 1940.

116. Ibid., December 9, 1939.

117. Kaplan, *Zora Neale Hurston*, 365.

118. Rawlings, *Cross Creek Cookery*, 184–85.

119. *Atlanta Daily World*, September 16, 1949.

120. *New York Amsterdam News*, September 27, 1947.

Chapter 3

121. Hurston, *Folklore*, 264.

122. Steve Brill and Evelyn Dean, *Identifying & Harvesting Edible and Medicinal Plants* (New York: HarperCollins, 2010), 7.

123. Frederick Douglass Opie interview with Dr. Nicole Farmer, May 2013.

124. Kaplan, *Zora Neale Hurston*, 48.

125. Audrey H. Ensminger, *Foods & Nutrition Encyclopedia*, vol. 1 (Boca Raton, FL: CRC Press, 1994), 28; Annette Kellerman, *Physical Beauty: How to Keep It* (n.p.: George H. Doran Company, 1918), 108.

126. Kaplan, *Zora Neale Hurston*, 495.

127. Hurston, *Folklore*, 266.

128. TNAU Agritech Portal, "Cereals: Rice," agritech.tnau.ac.in/postharvest/pht_rice_valueaddtn.html (March 27, 2013).

129. James A. Duke, *Handbook of Medicinal Herbs* (Boca Raton, FL: CRC Press, Inc., 1985), 133–34.

130. Hurston, *Folklore*, 266.

131. Opie interview with Farmer, August 2013.

132. Ibid., May 2013.

133. Hurston, *Folklore*, 514.

134. Duke, *Handbook of Medicinal Herbs*, ii.

135. Hurston, *Their Eyes Were Watching God*, 114.

136. Ibid.

137. Ibid., 116.

138. Hurston, *Folklore*, 266.

139. Ibid., 266.

140. Joseph Hawkins, *A History of a Voyage to the Coast of Africa* (New York: printed by the author for Luther Pratt, 1797), 134; Michel Adanson, *A Voyage to Senegal, the Isle of Goreé and the River Gambia* (London: J. Nourse [etc.], 1759) in John Pinkerton, *A General Collection of the Best and Most Interesting Voyages and Travels in All Parts of the World...* (London, 1813), Vol. 16, 618; Hurston, *Folklore*, 264.

141. *Chicago Defender*, November 30, 1929.

142. Ibid.

143. Hurston, *Folklore*, 265.

144. Duke, *Handbook of Medicinal Herbs*, 271–72; United States Department of Agriculture, "Rose," www.fs.usda.gov/detail/ipnf/learning/?cid=fsm9_019141.

145. Duke, *Handbook of Medicinal Herbs*, 273.

146. Caitlyn Scott, "Medicinal Plant: The Japanese Honeysuckle" (2008), mason.gmu.edu/~cscottm/plants.html#two.

147. Hurston, *Folklore*, 264.

148. Virginia Tech, "Weed Identification Guide," www.ppws.vt.edu/scott/weed_id/paqin.htm.

149. Faith Chandler, "What Are the Differences in Ribbon Cane & Sugar Cane Syrup?," eHow Food, www.ehow.com/info_8289705_differences-cane-sugar-cane-syrup.html; Fain's Honey, "Fain's Ribbon Cane Syrup," www.fainshoney.com/rib; Frederick Douglass Opie, "'Molasses-Colored Glasses': WPA and Other Sundry Sources on Molasses and Southern Foodways," *Southern Cultures* 14, no. 1 (Spring 2008): 84–86.

150. C.M. Brown Nurseries, Inc., "Our History," www.cmbrown.com/aboutus.htm (March 27, 2013); Anne Charlton, "Medicinal Uses of Tobacco in History," *Journal of the Royal Society of Medicine* 97, no. 4 (June 2004), accessed March 27, 2013, PMCID: PMC1079499; Brian Inglis, *The Forbidden Game: A Social History of Drugs* (New York: Charles Scribner's Sons, 1975), 39; Gene Borio, "Tobacco Timeline: The 17th Century—The Great Age of the Pipe," Tobacco.org, archive.tobacco.org/resources/history/tobacco_history17.html.

151. Charlton, "Medicinal Uses of Tobacco in History"; C.M. Brown Nurseries, Inc., "Our History."

152. I.U. Ibeme, "Medicinal Uses of Kanwu (or Akanwu) in Nigeria," www.scribd.com/doc/35463807/Medicinal-Uses-of-Kanwa-or-Akanwu-in-Nigeria (March 27, 2013); Mark Adwood, "7 Little Known Facts about Flax Seeds," UTI Cures, www.uticures.com/little-known-facts-about-flax-seeds (March 27, 2013).

153. MedlinePlus, "Potassium Carbonate Poisoning," www.nlm.nih.gov/medlineplus/ency/article/002481.htm.

154. Hurston, *Their Eyes Were Watching God*, 253.

155. Ibid., 249.

156. Hurston, *Folklore*, 266.

157. Herbal Medicine from Your Garden (Or Windowsill), "Sheep's Sorrel Is High in Vitamin C and Anti-Inflammatory" (December 15, 2009), www.herbalmedicinefromyourgarden.com/sheeps-sorrel-health-benefits.

158. Duke, *Handbook of Medicinal Herbs*, 271–72; Legends of America, "Herbs and Healing Properties," www.legendsofamerica.com/na-herbs8.html.

159. Barbi Trejo, "Fig Leaves Provide a Natural Health Remedy for Diabetes," *Natural News* (September 18, 2009), www.naturalnews.com/027050_figs_health_natural.html.

160. Botanical.com, "Ivy, Poison," botanical.com/botanical/mgmh/i/ivypoi17.html.

161. *Atlanta Daily World*, March 8, 1942.

162. Hurston, *Folklore*, 266.

163. Ibid.

164. Duke, *Handbook of Medicinal Herbs*, 319–21.

165. Opie interview with Farmer, May 2013.

166. University of Maryland Medical Center, "Aluminum Chloride (on the Skin)," www.umm.edu/drug/notes/Aluminum-chloride-On-the-skin.htm; WiseGeek, "What Are the Medical Uses of Alum?" www.wisegeek.org/what-are-the-medical-uses-of-alum.htm; About Religion, "Alum—Bai Fan," taoism.about.com/od/herbsforexternaluse/g/Bai_Fan.htm.

CHAPTER 4

167. Pieter de Marees, *Description and Historical Account of the Gold Kingdom of Guinea (1602)*, translated from the Dutch and edited by Albert van Dantzig and Adam Jones (New York: Oxford University Press, 1987), 54.

168. Ibid., 42.

169. Ibid., 181.

170. [Africanus] pseudo., *Remarks on the Slave Trade, and the Slavery of the Negroes in a Series of Letters* (London: J. Phillips [etc.], 1788). Microfilm edition (Sterling Memorial Library, Yale University, Microfilm # 13728.0-1), 14.

171. Theodore Canot, *Captain Canot or Twenty Years of an African Slaver: Being an Account of His Career and Adventures on the Coast, in the Interior, on Shipboard, and in the West Indies, Written Out and Edited from the Captain's Journals, Memoranda and Conversations* (first edition, New York: D. Appleton & Co., 1854); reprint, *Adventures of an African Slaver* (New York: Dover Publications, Inc., 1969), 160.

172. Helen Mendes, *The African Heritage Cookbook* (New York: Macmillan Company, 1971), 38–40.

173. Robert W. July, *Precolonial Africa: An Economic and Social History* (New York: Charles Scribner's Sons, 1975), 190.

174. De Marees, *Description and Historical Account*, 63.

175. July, *Precolonial Africa*, 190.

176. Alfred W. Crosby Jr., *The Columbian Exchange: Biological and Cultural Consequences of 1492*, foreword by Otto von Mering (Westport, CT: Greenwood Press, 1973), 75–77.

177. Ibid., 95–96.

178. Sam Bowers Hilliard, *Hog Meat and Hoecake: Food Supply in the Old South, 1840–1860* (Carbondale: Southern Illinois University Press, 1972), 46–47.

179. Ibid.

180. J.B. Moreton, "Manners and Customs in the West India Islands," London, 1790, 152–53, 155–58, in *After Africa: Extracts from British Travel Accounts and Journals of the Seventeenth, Eighteenth, and Nineteenth Centuries Concerning the Slaves, Their Manners, and Customs in the British West Indies*, introduction and edited by Roger D. Abrahams and John F. Szwed, assisted by Leslie Baker and Adrian Stackhouse (New Haven, CT: Yale University Press, 1983), 290.

181. George Juan and Antonio De Ulloa [Captains of the Spanish Navy, Fellows of the Royal Society of London and Royal Society of Paris], "A Voyage to South America," in *A General Collection of the Best and Most Interesting Voyages and Travels in All Parts of the World...* by John Pinkerton (London, 1813), 14, 602.

182. Eugene D. Genovese, *Roll Jordan Roll: The World the Slaves Made*, 1st edition, 1972 (New York: Vintage Books, 1976), 543.

183. Psyche A. Williams-Forson, *Building Houses Out of Chicken Legs: Black Women, Food, and Power* (Chapel Hill: University of North Carolina Press, 2006), 32.

184. Ibid.

185. Kaplan, *Zora Neale Hurston*, 228.

186. Ibid., 229.

187. Ibid.

188. Ibid.

189. Ibid.

190. Hurston, *Folklore*, 571.

191. *Baltimore Afro-American*, July 16, 1932.

192. *New Journal and Guide*, March 28, 1936.

193. *Pittsburgh Courier*, February 19, 1949.

194. Hurston, *Folklore*, 575.

195. Hurston, *Their Eyes Were Watching God*, 25, 144–45.

196. W.E.B. Du Bois, *The Souls of Black Folk* (New York: Barnes and Nobles Classic, 2003), 52.

197. Hurston, *Folklore*, 571.

198. James Weldon Johnson, *Along This Way: The Autobiography of James Weldon Johnson* (New York: Viking Press, 1933), 107–9.

199. Zora Neale Hurston, *Color Struck* [online] (Alexandria, VA: Alexander Street Press, LLC, 2012), 13.

200. James C. Scott, *Domination and the Arts of Resistance: The Hidden Transcripts* (New Haven, CT: Yale University Press, 1990), 183–85, 199–200.

201. Abby Fisher, *What Mrs. Fisher Knows About Old Southern Cooking* (San Francisco: Women's Co-op Printing Office, 1881), 19–20.

202. Hurston, *Folklore*, 20.

203. Ibid., 22.

204. Congo Cookbook, "Zanzibar Pilau," www.congocookbook.com/rice_recipes/zanzibar_pilau.html; Dixie Dining, "Bogged Down Along the SC Coast—And Loving It!" www.dixiedining.com/folklore.htm#chickenbog.

205. Rawlings, *Cross Creek Cookery*, 131.

206. Hurston, *Folklore*, 693.

207. Ibid., 22.

208. Ibid., 725–26.

209. Ibid., 816.

210. Ibid., 132–33.

211. Ibid., 894.

212. Williams-Forson, *Building Houses Out of Chicken Legs*, 18–20.

213. Ibid., 39, 45.

214. Ibid., 49.

215. Frederick Douglass Opie interview with Dr. Rodney Ellis, summer 2005; Frederick Douglass Opie interview with nutritionist Joan B. Lewis, summer 2005.

216. Frederick Douglass Opie interview with Lamenta Crouch, 2005.

Chapter 5

217. Frederick Douglass Opie interview with Dr. Elijah Saunders, summer 2005; Opie interview with Ellis.

218. Hurston, *Folklore*, 765.

219. Ibid., 107.

220. Ibid., 929.

221. *Chicago Daily Tribune*, March 6, 1931.

222. Hurston, *Folklore*, 929.

223. Opie, *Hog and Hominy*, 3.

224. Robert Tomson, "Voyage to the West Indies and Mexico (1555–1558)," in *Colonial Travelers in Latin America*, edited with an introduction by Irving A. Leonard (New York: Alfred A. Knopf, 1972), 58.

225. Opie, *Hog and Hominy*, 24.

226. Genovese, *Roll Jordan Roll*, 549.

227. Louis Hughes, *Thirty Years a Slave from Bondage to Freedom: The Institution of Slavery as Seen on the Plantation and in the Home of the Planter* (Milwaukee, WI: South Side Printing Company, 1897), 50.

228. Hurston, *Folklore*, 84.

229. Hurston, *Their Eyes Were Watching God*, 62.

230. *Chicago Daily Tribune*, March 6, 1931.

231. Box A18 (Alabama Barbecue), WPA Records, Library of Congress.

232. Box A830 (Arkansas Candidate's Barbecue), WPA Records, Library of Congress.

233. Box A157 (Monroe, Louisiana Barbecue), WPA Records, Library of Congress; Erwin Duke Stephens, Rare Book, Manuscript and Special Collections Library, Duke University; Recipetips.com, "Grilling or Smoking Wood," www.recipetips.com/glossary-term/t--37486/grilling-or-smoking-wood.asp.

234. Box A157 (Monroe, Louisiana Barbecue), WPA Records, Library of Congress; Stephens, Rare Book, Manuscript and Special Collections Library, Duke University; Recipetips.com, "Grilling or Smoking Wood."

235. Hurston, *Their Eyes Were Watching God*, 62.

236. Box A830 (Arkansas Candidate's Barbecue), WPA Records, Library of Congress.

237. *Atlanta Constitution*, July 19, 1940.

238. Dixon G. Hollingsworth Jr., "The Story of Barbecue," *Georgia Historical Quarterly* 63, no. 3 (Fall 1979): 391–95.

239. Box A18 (Alabama Barbecue), WPA Records, Library of Congress.

240. Hurston, *Their Eyes Were Watching God*, 62.

241. Hughes, *Thirty Years a Slave*, 48–49.

242. Ibid.

243. Martha McCulloch-Williams, *Dishes and Beverages of the Old South* (n.p.: McBride, Nast, 1913), 273.

244. Ibid., 274–75.

245. Ibid.

246. *Baltimore Afro-American*, May 3, 1941.

247. Box A830 (Arkansas Candidate's Barbecue), WPA Records, Library of Congress.

248. Box A18 (Alabama Barbecue), WPA Records, Library of Congress.

249. Stephens, Rare Book, Manuscript and Special Collections Library, Duke University.

250. *Chicago Daily Tribune*, June 23, 1928.

251. Box A157 (Monroe, Louisiana Barbecue), WPA Records, Library of Congress.

252. *New York Times*, June 21, 1938.

253. Michael Matsos interview by Amy Evans for the Southern Foodways Alliance, October 3, 2006.

254. Ibid.

255. *Baltimore Afro-American*, May 3, 1941.

256. Adapted from Chef Otis of Bon Goo on St. Nicholas Avenue in Harlem.

257. *Baltimore Afro-American*, May 3, 1941.

258. *Atlanta Daily World*, March 8, 1942.

259. Ibid.

260. Hurston, *Seraph on the Suwanee*, 72.

261. Ibid.

262. *Atlanta Constitution*, June 20, 1925.

263. Hurston, *Folklore*, 90.

264. *Atlanta Constitution*, June 20, 1925.

265. Alice Walker, *The Color Purple* (New York: Washington Square Press, 1983), 71.

266. Ibid., 73.

267. Ibid., 74.

268. Ibid., 82.

269. Hurston, *Folklore*, 50.

270. Ibid., 84.

271. Anne Yentsch, "Excavating the South's African American Food History," in *African American Foodways: Explorations of History and Culture*, edited by Anne L. Bower. The Food Series. (Urbana and Chicago: University of Illinois Press, 2007), 84.

272. Zora Neale Hurston, *Cold Keener* [online] (Alexandria, VA: Alexander Street Press, LLC, 2012), 22.

273. Hurston, *Folklore*, 95; Hurston, *Cold Keener*, 22.

274. Recipe adapted from Rawlings, *Cross Creek Cookery*, 159–61.

275. *Atlanta Daily World*, August 8, 1936.

276. *Chicago Defender*, July 9, 1949.

277. Florida slaw is of the Nancy Carter collection of "tested recipes." Carter was the director of home economics at Colonial Stores, Inc. in Atlanta, Georgia. *Atlanta Daily World*, January 20, 1956.

AFTERWORD

278. Andrew Apter, "On African Origins: Creolization and Connaissance in Haitian Vodou," *American Ethnologist* 29, no. 2 (Summer 2002): 233, 234, 245, 251, 256–60; Erwan Diantelli, "Deterriolization and Reterriolization of the Orisha Religion in Africa and the New World," *International Journal of Urban & Regional Research* 26, no. 1 (2002): 121–36; Ina J. Fandrich, "Yorùbá Influences on Haitian Vodou and New Orleans Voodoo," *Journal of Black Studies* 37, no. 5 (Summer 2007): 775–88; Yvonne Daniel, *Dancing Wisdom: Embodied Knowledge in Haitian Vodou, Cuban Yoruba, and Bahian Candomblé* (Urbana: University of Illinois Press, 2005), 5–13; Michelle A. Gonzales, *Afro-Cuban Theology: Religion, Race, Culture, and Identity* (Gainesville: University Press of Florida, 2006), 87, 88, 89; Keznas Filan, *The Haitian Vodou Handbook: Protocols for Riding with the Lwa* (Rochester, VT: Lake Book Manufacturing, 2007), 31, 32, 33, 34, 35; Nathaniel Samuel Murrel, *Afro-Caribbean Religions: An Introduction to Their Historical, Cultural, and Sacred Traditions* (Philadelphia: Temple University Press, 2010), 7, 8, 10, 30, 31, 32, 33.

279. William Allen and T.R.H. Thomson, *A Narrative of the Expedition to the River Niger in 1841*, vol. 1 (London: Richard Bentley, New Burlington Street, 1848; reprint, London: Frank Cass & Co. LTD., 1968), 118–19.

280. Hurston, *Folklore*, 424.

281. Filan, *Haitian Vodou Handbook*, 32, 33.

282. Daniel, *Dancing Wisdom*, 5–13; Murrel, *Afro-Caribbean Religions*, 135, 138, 140, 144.

283. George Eaton Simpson, "Four Vodun Ceremonies," *Journal of American Folklore* 59, no. 232 (April–June 1946): 155, 161–62.

284. Gay Wilentz, "If You Surrender to the Air: Folk Legends of Flight and Resistance in African American Literature," *MELUS* 16, no. 1, Folklore and Orature (Spring 1989–Spring 1990): 21–23; Wendy W. Walters, "'One of Dese Mornings, Bright and Fair,/Take My Wings and Cleave De Air': The Legend of the Flying Africans and Diasporic Consciousness," *MELUS* 22, no. 3, Varieties of Ethnic Criticism (Autumn 1997).

285. Walters, "One of Dese Mornings," 12.

286. Hurston, *Folklore*, 388.

287. Ibid., 404.

288. Ibid., 388.

289. Ibid., 411.

290. Ibid., 502.

291. Simpson, "Four Vodun Ceremonies," 55.

292. Odette M. Rigaud, Alfred Métraux and Rhoda Métraux, "The Feasting of the Gods in Haitian Vodu," *Primitive Man* 19, nos. 1–2 (January–April 1946): 55.

293. Hurston, *Folklore*, 511.

294. Rigaud, Métraux and Métraux, "Feasting of the Gods," 13–14.

295. Hurston, *Folklore*, 511–12.

296. Ibid., 512.

297. Ibid.

298. Ibid., 393.

299. *Baltimore Sun*, October 2, 1949.

300. Hurston, *Folklore*, 858.

301. Ibid., 393.

302. Ibid., 404.

303. Ibid., 432.

304. Ibid., 495.

305. Rigaud, Métraux and Métraux, "Feasting of the Gods," 52.

306. Simpson, "Four Vodun Ceremonies," 155.

307. Hurston, *Folklore*, 393, 432.

308. Ibid., 393, 495.

309. Rigaud, Métraux and Métraux, "Feasting of the Gods," 52; Simpson, "Four Vodun Ceremonies," 155.

310. Hurston, *Folklore*, 524.

311. Ibid., 312.

312. Ibid., 381, 389, 502.

313. Ibid., 176.

314. Ibid., 183.

315. Daniel, *Dancing Wisdom*, 150.

316. Martha L. Finch, "Food, Taste, and American Religions," *Religion Compass* (2010): 44.

317. David H. Brown, "Thrones of the Orichas: Afro-Cuban Altars in New Jersey, New York, and Havana," *African Arts* 26, no. 4 (October 1993): 51; Rigaud, Métraux and Métraux, "Feasting of the Gods," 58.

318. Simpson, "Four Vodun Ceremonies," 155, 161–62.

319. Rigaud, Métraux and Métraux, "Feasting of the Gods," 13–14; Finch, "Food, Taste, and American Religions," 44.

INDEX

W

ABOUT THE AUTHOR

F rederick Douglass Opie is a professor of history and foodways at Babson College and the author of *Hog and Hominy: Soul Food from Africa to America*; *Black Labor Migration in Caribbean Guatemala, 1882–1923*; and *Upsetting the Apple Cart: Black and Latino Coalitions in New York from Protest to Public Office*. Opie is a regular contributor on the radio show *The Splendid Table*.

Visit us at
www.historypress.net

This title is also available as an e-book

CPSIA information can be obtained
at www.ICGtesting.com
Printed in the USA
LVHW070951020222
710051LV00013B/329